weekends for trout fishing

IN NEW ZEALAND

Colin Moore

NEW
HOLLAND

First published in 2002 by New Holland Publishers (NZ) Ltd
Auckland • Sydney • London • Cape Town

218 Lake Road, Northcote, Auckland, New Zealand
14 Aquatic Drive, Frenchs Forest, NSW 2086, Australia
86–88 Edgware Road, London W2 2EA, United Kingdom
80 McKenzie Street, Cape Town 8001, South Africa

www.newhollandpublishers.com

ISBN 1-86966-013-7

Publishing manager: Renée Lang
Design: Graeme Leather
Editor: Mike Wagg
Maps: Nick Keenleyside

A catalogue record for this book is available from
the National Library of New Zealand.

Colour reproduction by PICA Colour Separation, Singapore
Printed by Kyodo Printing, Singapore

1 3 5 7 9 10 8 6 4 2

While the author and publishers have made every effort to ensure the information
in this book was correct at the time of going to press, they accept no responsibility
for any errors that may have occurred or for any injury or inconvenience that may
result from following the information contained herein. Facilities, locations, route
conditions or amenities can change over time, so it is recommended that the reader
call the operator or service and confirm any information that might be required.

contents

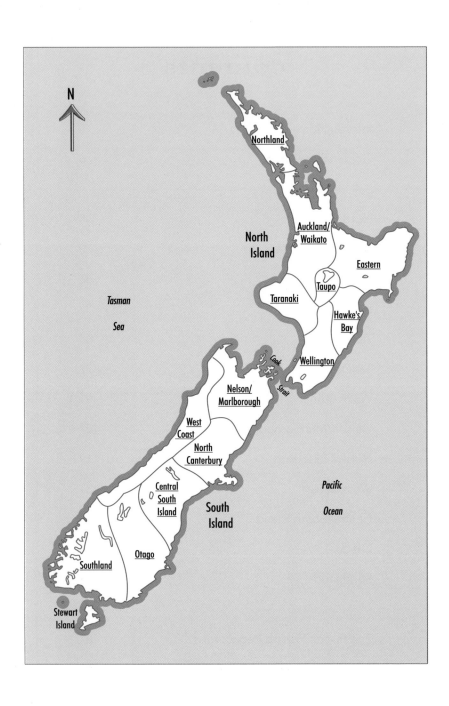

introduction

Some 350 years ago Izaak Walton's classic book *The Compleat Angler* transformed angling from being mere fish catching into an art. Wrote the acknowledged father of trout fishing: 'No life, my honest Scholar, no life so happy and so pleasant, as the life of a well governed Angler; for when the Lawyer is swallowed up with business, and the Statesman is preventing or contriving plots, then we sit on Cowslip-banks, hear the birds sing, and possess ourselves in as much quietness as these silent silver streams, which we now see glide so quietly by us.'

Walton's art began in New Zealand in 1867 with a shipment to the Canterbury Acclimatisation Society of brown trout from Tasmania that were descended from ova shipped from England in 1864. Rainbow trout arrived in February 1883 with a shipment of ova to the Auckland Acclimatisation Society from a hatchery on the Sonoma Creek, near San Francisco Bay, California.

The progeny from these importations have spread throughout New Zealand so that today wherever there is clean freshwater, from the Far North to the Deep South, you can be almost certain there will be trout.

The traditions of trout fishing were imported along with the fish, too. Angling for trout in New Zealand essentially remains the art that Walton described. But New Zealand has also developed traditions of its own, the most significant being to reject the notion of private waters. Another New Zealand peculiarity that retains the purity of trout fishing, as Walton conceived it, is that trout can neither be farmed nor bought or sold. In New Zealand if you want trout, you have to catch it yourself – from any one of the 12 regions administered by the New Zealand Fish and Game Council, all covered by a single fishing licence. The exception is the Taupo fishery, which requires a separate licence.

Weekends for Trout Fishing is divided into matching regions and as the title suggests, it is intended as a guide for planning a trip to those 'Cowslip-banks leaving Lawyers swallowed up in business'. More than anything, trout fishing is the perfect reason to take a break from normal routines.

guide to

 Where and What

For further information and updates to regulations, please contact the relevant regional Fish and Game New Zealand office. Contact details can be found in the Information section in each chapter.

 Casting Around

This guide is not intended to be an exhaustive guide to all trout fishing spots; its emphasis is on rivers, lakes and streams that are accessible and cover a range of levels.

 Guides and Charters

If you are looking for specialist support in whatever form, this list will put you in touch with some of the individuals and organisations in each region.

 Tackle Box

As the name suggests, a good range of fishing-related equipment is on offer from these retailers and service providers.

our guide

 ## Catch a Meal
The restaurants and cafés featured in this guide have been selected because they offer variety and are generally within easy reach of the fishing spots and accommodation featured.

 ## Hang your Hook
The hotels and lodges, some of which are world class, and farmstays, homestays and bed and breakfast establishments listed within this guide have been chosen because of their proximity to the fishing spots featured. Some also have special interest to those wanting a total fishing experience.

 ## When the Fish Don't Bite
Not everyone wants to fish all day, every day, so included under this heading is a selection of summer and winter recreational activities, many of which are suitable for families, and some of which are unique to a specific region.

Maps
Please note that the maps in this book are not intended to take the place of those published by Fish and Game New Zealand or indeed any other commercially produced maps. Their main purpose is to indicate the approximate location of most recommended fishing spots. Regional boundaries and all streams, rivers and lakes are not necessarily detailed.

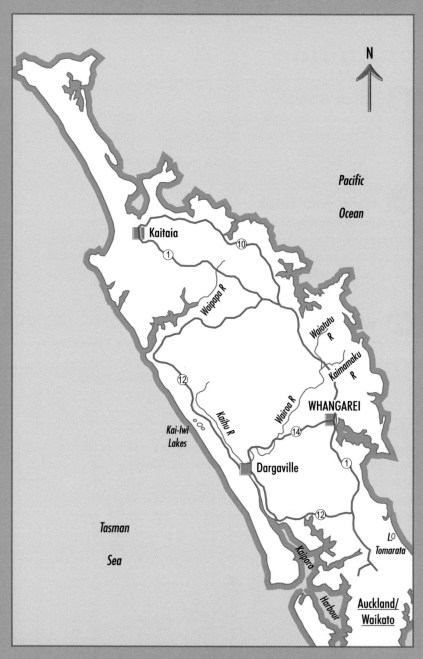

Northland

Northland prides itself as the 'winterless north', which means that by rights trout, which are suited to colder, more oxygenated water, should have about as much chance of surviving north of Wellsford as a snowball on Ninety Mile Beach. Fortunately for fishers who enjoy a bit of sunshine too, trout seem an extremely adaptable species – or at least those nurtured by passionate Northland fishers are. Against all conventional acclimatisation wisdom, trout not only live happily in some winterless waters but in places even prosper into the trophy category. Rainbow trout have generally acclimatised better to the warmer conditions than brown trout, but you will still find good-sized browns in cooler, wooded streams.

There are no big rivers in Northland – perhaps it doesn't rain enough – but there is no shortage of clear water flowing past shady banks in the wilderness. For instance, the Waipapa River which rises in the Puketi Forest near Kerikeri and empties into the upper reaches of the Hokianga Harbour, makes as quiet and peaceful a river ramble as you will find anywhere in the Northland bush wilderness. It also holds wild trout throughout its entire length that average about 0.5 kg. The Kerikeri River, with its headwaters just over the hill from the beginnings of the Waipapa, flows in the other direction until it exits into the Kerikeri Inlet near the historic Stone Store.

FAMOUS FOR

- Big game fishing
- Diving at the Poor Knights Islands
- Sailing in the Bay of Islands
- Sea kayaking at Whangaroa
- Waipoua Kauri Forest
- Ninety Mile Beach
- Ruawai, the kumara capital

- The fish-and-chip shop at Manganui
- Waitangi Marae – site of the Treaty signing in 1840
- Surf beaches
- Hundertwasser-designed toilets at Kawakawa
- Cape Reinga Lighthouse – New Zealand's northernmost point

INFORMATION

New Zealand Fish and Game
Northland Region
72 Robert Street
PO Box 1099, Whangarei
09 438 4135
rhoetjex@clear.net.nz
www.fishandgame.org.nz
Manager: Rudi Hoetjes
Field Officer: Graham White

Destination Northland
PO Box 365
Paihia
09 402 7683
northland@xtra.co.nz
www.northland.co.nz
www.twincoast.co.nz

Whangarei Visitor Information Centre
92 Otaika Road
09 438 1079
www.whangareinz.org.nz

Kauri Coast Visitor Information Centre
54 Normanby Street
Dargaville
0800 528 744

Hokianga Visitor Information Centre
State Highway 12
Omapere
09 405 8869
www.hokianga.co.nz

What many visitors to this subtropical fruit-growing region probably don't realise is that the progeny of trout stocks released throughout Northland in the 1960s and 1970s are now self-sustaining, and in the upper reaches of the Kerikeri River, above State Highway 10, grow to up to 1.5 kg. And the Bay of Islands and the Treaty House at Waitangi are almost within casting distance.

By far the best-known and most productive trout fishery in Northland is the Kai-Iwi Lakes, near Dargaville. The lakes are in sand dune, with pine forests to the water's edge. They are also quite deep with sudden drop-offs – which is just where rainbows of up to 4.5 kg may lie. Many of Auckland's top anglers rate fly fishing a Kai-Iwi drop-off with a fast-sinking line and a koura or bully imitation to be among the best lake fishing you will find anywhere in the country. The lakes are on the western loop of the Twin Coast Discovery Highway and just up the road is the Waipoua Kauri Forest.

Northland may not be the country's most noted trout fishery, but when you cast a fly or spinner in the Northland region you are never far from a top holiday spot, for a weekend or a week. Tutukaka, the Bay of Islands and Whangaroa are internationally renowned game fishing centres, but many charter boat skippers will enjoy hosting anglers using saltwater fly rods.

WHERE AND WHAT

The Northland Fish and Game region extends north from a line between Wellsford and Mangawhai Heads to Cape Reinga and North Cape. Regular releases by the former Acclimatisation Societies in the region in the 1960s and 1970s has established a good base, mostly self-sustaining, of trout that have adapted to Northland's subtropical climate. The wild stream and river fishery is supplemented each year in five bodies of water – two reservoirs and three sand lakes – by an annual stocking of 4000 rainbow trout fingerlings. The fishing terrain is varied and may be tree-lined or through farmland.

The Northland fishing regulations follow the general North Island regulations. All lakes and reservoirs in the region are open year-round. Rivers and streams are open from 1 October to 31 April, with a closed season from 1 May to 30 September. Bait may not be used in any rivers or streams. The bag limit in rivers and streams is two fish. The limit for lakes and reservoirs is three fish. The minimum length is 300 mm.

Casting 🎣 around

LAKES AND RESERVOIRS

Kai-Iwi Lakes

The Kai-Iwi lakes are 35 km north of Dargaville. The Lakes, which in Maori roughly translates to 'Kai' (for food) and 'Iwi' (for tribe), are famous in the north for their scenery. The fishing is popular throughout the winter, but still provides good numbers of fish all year round. During summer, boating tactics are used, as the fish tend to inhabit the deeper margins of these lakes when water temperatures are warm.

The lakes hold rainbow trout and every year produce well-conditioned fish that can grow up to 4–4.5 kg. The main types of tackle used are fast sinking lines with koura or bully imitation flies for shore-based anglers, or lead lines and jigs for boat-based fishermen.

Whau Valley Dam

This man-made dam serves as Whangarei's public water supply, and as such can vary in depth and size. Annually stocked with 300 rainbow fingerlings, it is essentially the nearest fishing anglers have in the Whangarei area. Angling is restricted to shore-based activity, with good results coming when using a sinking line. Fish targeted are rainbows, but browns are also present and have managed to self-sustain from early liberations. The rainbows tend to average 1 kg while the browns are large but hard to catch.

Lake Manuwai

Lake Manuwai is an irrigation dam a few kilometres north of Waipapa which serves the Kerikeri horticultural belt. It also holds good numbers of rainbow trout, which are readily taken with wet flies and bait. Normal shore-based fishing techniques work well and non-motorised boat fishing is permitted. The lake-edge vegetation impedes angling in a lot of places but fishing is good where areas permit. The lake is set in a very picturesque valley catchment and is a great place for the whole family.

RIVERS AND STREAMS

Northland has hundreds of kilometres of fishable streams and rivers with wild populations of rainbow and brown trout. While not as spectacular as some waters elsewhere in the country they can provide great fishing, particularly for those anglers prepared to go exploring. Rivers and streams can hold 3 kg-plus fish, with the average being around 1 kg.

Waima River

The Waima River is 45 km north of Dargaville along State Highway 12, then up Donnellys Road to Donnelleys Crossing. Fly fishing usually produces the best results in these waters and they are best suited to the more experienced and active angler.

Kaihu River

The Kaihu River is 30 km north of Dargaville on State Highway 12 and flows south. The best place to start fishing this river is upstream from Kaihu settlement. The river tends to run clear most of the time and is very picturesque.

Mangatu River

The Mangatu River flows into the Kaihu River about 5 km upstream of the motor camp along Oputeke Road. The conditions are similar to those of the Kaihu River.

Punakitere River

The Punakitere River has a small population of rainbow trout in its upper reaches. This river can be reached by travelling west through Kaikohe and then south down Matarua Road for 8 km until you reach the first main bridge.

GUIDES AND CHARTERS

Sportfishing Charters
Tutukaka
09 434 3233

Bream Bay Charters
Bream Bay
09 432 7484

Tutukaka Charters
Tutukaka Marina
Marina Road, Tutukaka
09 434 3818
fish@clear.net.nz
www.sportfishing.co.nz

Freedom Fishing Charters
Opito Bay Road
RD1 Kerikeri
09 407 5516

Stealaway Charters
14 Kotare Street
Ahipara
09 409 4007

Millennium Fishing Charters
Kent Street
Whangaroa
09 405 0995

The more successful flies in this river are Parson's Glory and rabbit flies.

Waitangi River

The Waitangi River flows east from Waimate North to Haruru Falls near Paihia. The river has a scattering of rainbows along its entire length. The best area to fish is around the Bay of Islands Holiday Park (Lilypond), Puketona Road, and Paihia. The river can be accessed east of Puketona Junction off SH10.

Waipapa River and Waihoanga Stream

The Waipapa River flows through the Puketi Kauri Forest and has wild trout throughout its entire length. This river can be accessed from State Highway 1 and Forest Road about 8 km north of Okaihau. These trout average about 0.5 kg and take smelt flies like Parson's Glory, a wide range of nymphs such as Pheasant Tail, Halfback, and Hare and Copper. In the summer months' imitations of cicada and green beetles work well. The scenery is the nearest Northland has to a back-country fishery.

Waipapa Stream

The Waipapa stream flows from Lake Manuwai and out to the Kerikeri inlet. The most productive areas to fish are near the State Highway 10 road bridge and downstream towards the coast. Anglers need landowner entry permission as most fishing is from private land.

TACKLE BOX

McCoy & Thomas Sports
1–3 Rust Ave
Whangarei
09 438 3111

Stirling Sports Whangarei
49 Vine Street
Whangarei
09 438 9951

Stumpy's Bait & Tackle
121 Riverside Road
Riverside
Whangarei
09 438 1565

Dargaville Sports
92 Victoria Street
Dargaville
09 439 8520

Keri Sportworld
Main Road
Kerikeri
09 407 8447

Bay Dive & Fishing Tackle
41 Kerikeri Road
Kerikeri
09 407 5585

Bay Rod & Reel Services
Cass Street
Russell
09 403 7995

Coopers Beach Sports
172 State Highway 10
Coopers Beach
Mangonui
09 406 0592

Kerikeri River

The Kerikeri River flows from the high plateau next to the Puketi State Forest down to the Kerikeri inlet. The fishing is best above State Highway 10 where rainbows of up to 1.5 kg can be caught, but landowner entry permission is required.

Tirohanga River

The Tirohanga is a small stream that flows down from the western side of the Russell State Forest and meanders towards the township of Kawakawa. The upper reaches don't hold fish but they are found once the river levels out. Access is through private property and landowner entry permission is required.

CATCH A MEAL

Blah, Blah, Blah Café and Bar
101 Victoria Street
Dargaville
09 439 6300
eclectic menu, gourmet pizzas

Tides Restaurant
Williams Road
Paihia
09 402 7557
tides_restaurant@yahoo.com
as good as it gets

Janit's Texas Diner
State Highway 10
Kaeo
09 405 0569
genuine Texas ribs and monster breakfast

Mangonui Fish-and-Chip Shop
State Highway 10
Mangonui
09 406 0478
voted best fish and chips in the country

Rocket Café
cnr Kerikeri Road and Cobham Road
Central Kerikeri
09 407 1050
citrusbar@xtra.co.nz
consistently voted best café in Northland

Killer Prawn
26–28 Bank Street
Whangarei
09 430 3333
www.killerprawn.co.nz
a splash of California, and prawns to die for

Dickens Inn
Quality Street Mall
Cameron St
Whangarei
09 430 0406
gmc@dickensinn.co.nz
www.dickensinn.co.nz
alfresco dining and an inviting atmosphere

Mangahahuru Stream

Situated 10 km north of Whangarei along State Highway 1 is the Mangahahuru Stream which suits the more experienced angler. The best fishing is found by walking upstream for about 3 km from a bridge on State Highway 1 (signposted), although there is reasonable fishing downstream too. Landowner entry permission is required.

Kirikiritoki Stream

Follow the Whananaki Road turn-off, about 20 km north of Whangarei on State Highway 1, for about 6 km until you reach a bridge over the Kirikiritoki Stream. From here, Marua Road winds alongside the stream for many kilometres, giving good access for anglers. This river is wooded along the banks and is probably more suited for experienced anglers. Approximately 2 km downstream from the Whananaki Road bridge the Kaikanui stream joins the Kirikiritoki Stream and there is good fishing for several kilometres downstream.

Kaikanui River

The first bridge on the Old Russell Road just off State Highway 1 at Whakapara, about 22 km from Whangarei, marks the lower end of the Kaikanui and the Kaimamaku Rivers. This is a very productive spot and well worth trying. Downstream from this point the river is known as the Whakapara River.

HANG YOUR HOOK

Northern Wairoa Hotel
Victoria Street
Dargaville
09 439 8923
solid 1922 hotel with modern services

Kauri House Lodge
Bowen Street
Dargaville
09 439 8082
kauri@informace.co.nz
19th-century villa with luxury private ensuite guest rooms – breakfast included

Acacia Lodge
57 Mill Bay Road
PO Box 60
Mangonui
Graeme.dunn@acacia.co.nz
www.acacia.co.nz
idyllic setting in historic Mangonui harbour

Cavalli Beach House
PO Box 690
Kerikeri
09 405 1049
www.cavallibeachouse.com
ultra-modern lodge with breathtaking views

Huntaway Lodge
Te Ngaere Bay
RD1 Kaeo
09 405 1611
greg@huntawaylodge.com
modern, cosy – super friendly hosts

HANG YOUR HOOK

Puketotara Luxury Lodge
PO Box 488
State Highway 10
Kerikeri
09 407 7780
relax@puketotaralodge.co.nz
www.puketotaralodge.co.nz
*nestled in 30 acres of orchards and
bush – meals available*

Villa Helios
44 Du Fresne Place
Tapeka Point, Russell
09 403 7229
villa.helios@xtra.co.nz
*romantic seaside setting with a
touch of the Greek Islands*

Kauri Cliffs
Matauri Bay Road
Matauri Bay
09 405 1900
info@kauricliffs.com
www.kauricliffs.com
*one of the most exclusive, and
expensive, in the country*

Parua House
Parua Bay
Whangarei Heads
09 436 5855
paruahomestay@clear.net.nz
*unobstructed bay views with
superb food and hospitality*

Kaimamaku River

The gravel-based river winds alongside the Old Russell Rd and in the summer the water is gin clear. This river is probably more suited to nymphing the pools as the water may be too warm in summer for fish to lie in the runs.

Whakapara River

This river, 22 km north of Whangarei on State Highway 1, has good fishing upstream from the main road to the junction of Kaimamaku/Kaikanui Rivers. Downstream there is excellent fishing for several kilometres.

Waiotu River

Also on State Highway 1, 28 km north of Whangarei, you will find the Waiotu beneath a road and railway bridge. There is good fishing up and downstream. If you go over the railway line and head back towards Whangarei, the first bridge you come to cross is the Puhipuhi Stream. Go downstream on the left bank and you will come to the junction of this stream with the Waiotu. If you keep going for about 4 km downstream you will come to the junction of the Whakapara/Waiotu Rivers. It is well worth trying here in the evening.

Waiariki River

A small river, which joins the Waiotu 0.5 km downstream on the left-hand bank. This junction is a good place at night and is reached along the Waiotu riverbanks by way of marginal strip. Fish in this waterway are generally browns, with rainbows in the lower 400 m before the Waiotu. Access to upper areas is through private land so entry permission is needed.

Wairua River

The Wairua River runs from the junction of the Waiotu/Whakapara Rivers north of Whangarei to Titoki some 26 km west of Whangarei. Access can be gained from many roads. There is good fishing, especially when casting to the evening rise. Another place to try is back along Rushbrook Road (off the Jordan Valley Road about 250 m left past Hikurangi on State Highway 1), where there is a bridge that crosses the Wairua River. Good fishing upstream and downstream. Farmer permission is required for access. The Wairua also has good fishing near Titoki. Some 2–3 km hold trout in pools and runs with some good fish to be taken. About 12 km along the Maungatapere–Kaikohe Road, reached off State Highway 14 to Dargaville, you will again cross the Wairua River, near the Wairua Falls. There is good fishing in the vicinity for both spinning and fly fishing.

Mangakahia River

From the Wairua River bridge keep driving towards Kaikohe for about 4 km. The Mangakahia River and its tributaries have had trout liberated in them, but trout do not seem to hold in the system. Fish seen in this river and its tributaries are usually mullet, and many a trout angler has been fooled, believing they are casting to a trout.

WHEN THE FISH DON'T BITE

The Kauri Museum
Church Road
Matakohe
09 431 7417
thekauri@xtra.co.nz
www.hmu.com/matakohe
Northland's kauri history revealed – open daily

Nocturnal Park
Fairburn Road
Kaitaia
09 408 410
glow-worms and kiwis – open daily

Ancient Kauri Kingdom
State Highway 1
Awanui
09 406 7122
akk@xtra.co.nz
www.ancientkauri.co.nz
crafted gems from 80,000 year-old swamp kauri

Paradise Connexion
Whitecaps Place
Hihi
PO Box 28, Mangonui
09 406 0460
full day tours to Cape Reinga from Doubtless Bay

New Zealand Sea Kayak Adventures
PO Box 454
Paihia
09 402 8596
nzkayak@clear.net.nz
sea kayaking in the Bay of Islands and beyond

Fullers Bay of Islands
Maritime Building
Paihia
09 402 7421

The Strand
Russell
09 403 7866

www.fullers-bay-of-islands.co.nz
Bay of Islands cruising to Cape Brett and the hole in the rock

Dolphin Discoveries
Marsden Road
PO Box 400
Paihia
09 402 8234
Dolphin@igrin.co.nz
www.dolphin.co.nz
swim with dolphins in the Bay of Islands

Poor Knights Dive Centre
Marina Road
Tutukaka
09 433 6803
www.diving.co.nz
dive at the Poor Knights or the wrecks of HMNZS Tui and HMNZS Waikato

Pakiri Beach Horse Rides
Rahuikiri Road
Pakiri
RD2 Wellsford
09 422 6275
Pakirihorse@xtra.co.nz
www.horseride-nz.co.nz
pony trekking in sublime coastal surroundings

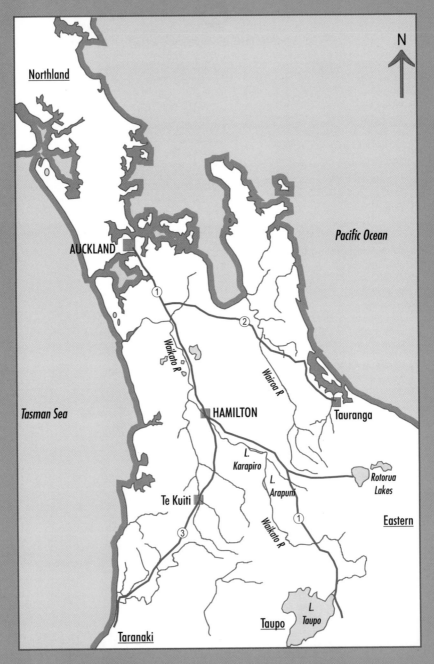

Auckland and Waikato

Probably half of the population of New Zealand lives in the Auckland and Waikato region. It's an area famed for yachting, dairy cows and breeding thoroughbred racehorses. There is excellent saltwater fishing in the Hauraki Gulf and on the region's west coast. And in the wilderness of the Coromandel and Kaimai Ranges there are wonderful tramping opportunities for those who want to get away from it all.

What may be less well known is that the region offers excellent opportunities for trout fishing too, with brown trout predominant in the Waikato and Waipa Rivers and mainly rainbows in the region's many other rivers. And given the number of trout fishers resident in Auckland and Hamilton, that should be good news for those who want a weekend away fishing without having to travel too far.

For instance, you can fish for trout at Lake Ototoa – just half an hour by car from downtown Auckland. This small, scenic lake, just north of Helensville on the South Kaipara heads, has benefited from the voluntary helping hands of Trout Unlimited and is regularly stocked with fast-maturing rainbow trout. There is good fishing when the water cools in late autumn and trout start feeding around the weed-beds. Fish of up to 2.5 kg have been taken here.

FAMOUS FOR

- Auckland, New Zealand's largest city
- The Harbour Bridge
- The Waitemata Harbour, home of the America's Cup
- Hauraki Gulf snapper
- Sky Tower
- The Waikato River – the country's longest
- Breeding thoroughbred race horses
- Waitomo glow-worm caves
- The Coromandel Peninsula
- Surf at Raglan

Not much further from the centre of the largest city in New Zealand there is a wild fishery river, the Wairoa, with 5 km of fishing water over a wadeable shingle bed. Another half-hour's drive and the fishing possibilities expand considerably along the Kauaeranga River on the Coromandel Peninsula and the vast Waikato and Waihou River systems.

But if such locations are just too far away to duck out to between business meetings, Lake Pupuke on Auckland's North Shore is certainly not. The deep suburban lake has an honoured place in New Zealand trout fishing because in 1883 the Auckland Acclimatisation Society liberated fry in the lake from among the first three importations of rainbow trout. And it was from healthy and vigorous 4 kg hens netted from Pupuke that rainbow stock were bred and first released in the Rotorua lakes 10 years later.

INFORMATION

Fish and Game Auckland/Waikato Region
Hilldale Game Park
Brymer Road
RD9 Hamilton
07 849 1666
www.fishandgame.org.nz
Manager: Doug Emmett

Auckland Visitor Information Centre
287 Queen Street
Auckland
09 979 2333
reservations@aucklandnz.com
www.aucklandnz.co.nz

Auckland Freshwater Anglers Club
PO Box 63016
Papatoetoe South

Tourism Waikato
PO Box 970
Hamilton
07 839 3360
info@waikato.tourism.co.nz
www.waikatonz.co.nz

Hamilton Visitor Information Centre
cnr Anglesea and Bryce Streets
Hamilton
07 839 3580
hamiltoninfo@wave.co.nz

Hamilton Anglers Club
PO Box 9036
Hamilton North

Tourism Coromandel
PO Box 592
Thames
0800 888 222
info@coromandel.tourism.co.nz
www.thecoromandel.com

Thames Visitor Information Centre
206 Pollen Street
Thames
07 868 7284
TMZvin@nzhost.co.nz

Tokoroa Freshwater Angling Club
PO Box 208
Tokoroa

The fishing from Pupuke's cowslip banks is not quite as 'excellent' or the fish as 'abundant' as the society reported in the 1892 season; but it continues to be stocked every year with large-growing strains of rainbow and brown yearlings from Lake Waikaremoana, and the water quality of the lake is constantly improving. A canoeist out early morning training claims to have seen rainbow trout up to 2.5 kg around the hospital jetty.

Other lakes regularly stocked near Auckland are Lake Tomarata, near Wellsford, and three sand-dune lakes near Waiuku: Muirs (Otamatearoa), Parkinsons and Thomsons (Whatihua). The fishing is not easy and landowner permission is required for access to Muirs, but it can be worth the trouble. Top angler Gary Kemsley is reported to have taken trout of 2.5 kg from Thomsons and 3.5 kg brown trout from Muirs.

Several hours from Auckland, at the far end of the region, there is excellent wilderness fishing – for both brown and rainbow trout – in the headwaters of the Whakapapa River. The river, flowing through native forests with rapids, deep pools and large boulder runs, is the antithesis of suburban Lake Pupuke and underlines the diversity available to trout fishers in the Auckland and Waikato region.

WHERE AND WHAT

The Auckland and Waikato Fish and Game region is one of the most extensive in the country, stretching from Lake Tomarata north of Auckland, south to the Mokau River on the border of Taranaki, east to include all of the Coromandel Peninsula, the Waikato River and hydro lakes system, and the upper reaches of the Wanganui River system, south-west of Lake Taupo. The diversity of the fishing is just as extensive. There are small, regularly stocked lakes near Auckland, while the Coromandel rivers and parts of the King Country provide some of the best wilderness fishing in New Zealand. Many of the Waikato streams and rivers run through open farmland.

Fishing conditions in the region are influenced by heavy rainfall in the upper catchments, and water clarity can be destroyed within a few hours of steady rain. When there has been heavy rain it pays to check river and stream water levels and conditions so you can assess fishing prospects before leaving home. This may take a little detective work with the telephone but it should not be too difficult to find an observant resident who lives near your selected fishing spot. For rivers in the Waikato, data for water levels for the last 7 days and flow rates are available online from www.ew.govt.nz/

The Auckland and Waikato fishing regulations follow the general North Island regulations. All lakes in the region are open all year. The rivers and streams open all year are the Hikutaia River downstream from the ford on the

Whangamata Track; Mangaotaki River downstream from the lower bridge on the Mangaotaki Road (Piopio); Mangawhio River between the Waikato River and the Falls; Marokopa River downstream from its confluence with the Mangatuahaua Stream; Ohinemuri River downstream from the Victoria Street bridge, at Waihi; Puniu River downstream from the Seafund Road bridge; Waihou River; Waikato River; Waimakariri Stream; Waipa River downstream from Toa Bridge (some 16 km upstream from Otorohanga); Wairoa River; Waitawheta Stream downstream from the upstream end of the public vehicle access on Franklin Road; Whanganui River downstream from its confluence with the Whakapapa River.

Waters closed from 30 June to 1 October are all rivers, streams and their tributaries which flow into but not including Lake Arapuni, Lake Waipapa, Lake Karapiro and that part of the Waikato River downstream from the Maraetai Dam to above the Karapiro Dam. The closed waters restrictions do not apply to the Mangawhio Stream and tributaries; Pokaiwhenua Stream and tributaries; Waipa Stream and tributaries; Waikato River; Waipapa River and tributaries. Trolling in the Waikato River between the Arapuni Dam and the upper limits of Lake Karapiro (as shown by the white marker post, situated 200 m below the Huihuitaha Stream mouth) is prohibited.

Fly fishing only waters in the region are Awakino River from its source to the Mahoenui Bridge; Hikutaia River from its source to the ford on the old Whangamata Track; Kakahu Stream (north-east of Okoroire); Kaniwhaniwha Stream; Komata Stream; Mangatutu Stream from its source to the Lethbridge Road bridge; Ngakoaohia Stream from its source to the bridge on the Pirongia–Kawhia Road; Okauaka Stream; Puniu River from its source to the Bayley Road bridge; Waione Stream; Waipapa River upstream from the first waterfall situated about 500 m from Lake Waipapa; Wairoa River from its source to the Hunua Falls.

The daily bag limit is two in the Awakino River; Lake Karapiro; the Waipa River and its tributaries upstream from the State Highway 3 bridge at Otorohanga; and the Whakapapa River and its tributaries upstream from the confluence with the Piopiotea Stream. There is no bag limit on the Waihou River and its tributaries upstream from Okoroire and the Waimakariri Stream and its tributaries, but only two trout may be longer than 30 cm. The daily limit in all other waters is five trout. The minimum length for trout taken is 30 cm in all waters except in the Waihou River upstream from Okoroire and the Waimakariri Stream where there is no minimum length.

Several pamphlets on trout fishing in the Auckland and Waikato region are available free from tackle shops or by sending a stamped, self-addressed envelope to Fish & Game New Zealand, Auckland/Waikato Region, RD 9, Hamilton.

Casting  around

WAIKATO RIVER AND HYDRO LAKES

Waikato River

The Waikato River, the longest in New Zealand, holds large numbers of trout. Browns are found throughout its length with rainbows plentiful upstream of Hamilton. The best fishing is generally at twilight or after dark. The lower river fishes best during the winter but there is good fishing in the upper reaches all year round. Popular spots include beneath the Karapiro Dam (track on western side), and the Karapiro Stream mouth at Cambridge. Riverside tracks in Hamilton and Cambridge give access to good fishing water.

Lake Karapiro

Good lake-shore fishing can be reached from Horahora Road. The most popular spots are the mouths of the Pokaiwhenua and Little Waipa Streams. There are boat-ramps off State Highway 1 and at the mouth of the Little Waipa Stream. Trophy fish with browns of nearly 4 kg are possible. Trolling is popular but weed can be a problem.

Lake Arapuni

This is the most popular lake fishery in the Auckland/Waikato region. It is heavily stocked with rainbow trout and anglers usually enjoy good catches. Most fish are rainbows but the browns are usually over 3 kg. Popular locations at the southern end of the lake for the shore-based anglers include below the Waipapa Dam, the mouth of the Tumai Stream (track from the eastern side of the Waipapa Dam) and the Mangawhio Stream (track from the boat-ramp located about 1 km downstream from the Waipapa Dam). At the northern end of the lake, you can reach several beaches from Landing Road. Many anglers also fish in the vicinity of the Arapuni and Waipapa Dams. There are five boat-ramps around the lake.

Pokaiwhenua Stream

A spring-fed stream with its source in the pine forests near Tokoroa. The reaches below the waterfall on the Putaruru–Arapuni Road, have a good spawning run of large trout from Lake Karapiro in autumn. Access is across farmland and landowners' permission is required.

Little Waipa Stream

A large spring-fed stream near Putaruru with an abundant trout population. Access is from Putaruru–Arapuni, Pearsons, or Old Taupo Roads. Good water that is rarely fished can also be reached across private farmland from Huihuitaha Road – it's well worth the extra effort.

WAIPA RIVER SYSTEM

Waipa River

The Waipa River is mostly fished above Otorohanga, where there is over 30 km of superb fishing water. From Otorohanga the river runs parallel to Otewa Road for about 16 km to Toa Bridge – the upstream limit for winter fishing. Above Toa Bridge the river is mainly accessed on foot. Access to the upper reaches is across private farmland from Owawenga Road.

Puniu River

The Puniu River is the largest tributary of the Waipa River, flowing through the Pureora Forest and joining the river at Pirongia. The Puniu River has 20 km of fishing water, mostly in the headwaters and middle reaches. Access is from Bayley, Newman and Duncan Roads.

Mangatutu Stream

A popular stream, south of Te Awamutu, that is heavily fished by local anglers. Pools and runs are plentiful and the clear banks make casting easy. Access is from the Wharepuhunga Road, which runs parallel to the Mangatutu Stream for 5 km.

TACKLE BOX

Tisdalls Outdoors
176 Queen Street
Auckland
09 379 0254

Mac's Sports
235 Alexandra Street
Te Awamutu
07 871 5300

Fish & Game Shop
96–98 Sunnybrae Road
Glenfield
Auckland
09 444 0023

Hunting and Fishing Westgate
7 Cabernet Crescent
West Harbour
Auckland
09 833 3019

Sportways Hunting & Fishing
431 Te Rapa Road
Hamilton
07 849 0297

R & R Sport
943 Victoria Street
Hamilton
07 839 3755

Fish'n Bits
9140 Parry Palm Ave
Waihi
07 863 6908

Hamill's
53 The Strand
Tauranga
07 578 0995

Moakurarua Stream

The Moakurarua Stream has its source in the steep hill country to the west of Otorohanga and flows north to join the Waipa River just south of Pirongia. The upper reaches of the Moakurarua have a clear gravel bottom, mostly wadeable, offering good fishing. Access is off the Otorohanga–Honikiwi or Otorohanga–Kawhia Roads.

Ngakoaohia Stream

Rising on Mt Pirongia, the Ngakoaohia Stream flows east to join the Waipa River. This small stream consists of pools and runs with a clear gravel bottom which lends itself well to nymph and dry fly fishing. Access is from the Pirongia–Kawhia Road.

Kaniwhaniwha Stream

A small shingle and boulder stream that runs through bush and farmland down the northern slopes of Mt Pirongia. Access is off the Limeworks Loop Road. The stream is mainly fished with nymph or dry fly during the summer.

Mangaokewa Stream

In its upper reaches the Mangaokewa flows through an extensive area of native forest. These waters are best suited for spin fishing and hold good-size rainbow and brown trout. Access is off the Mangaokewa Road and from the scenic Mangaokewa Reserve just south of Te Kuiti.

WAIHOU RIVER SYSTEM

Waihou River

The Waihou River system runs for 160 km from the Mamaku Plateau down the eastern side of the Waikato region to the Firth of Thames. Most fishing in the Waihou is in the upper reaches above Okoroire where the river is crystal clear – classic dry fly waters. In this section of the river trout numbers are exceptionally high – mainly small fish, though recent drift dive surveys have seen reasonable numbers of large rainbows. Access is from the Hamilton–Rotorua highway, Whites Road (road between SH5 and SH1), and at Okoroire behind the Hotel.

Waiomou Stream

An upper tributary of the Waihou with about 10 km of fishable water. This is a popular river with a high catch-rate. Three tributaries of the Waiomou – the Omahine, Rapurapu, and the Kakahu Streams – offer good, small stream fly fishing. Access is off the Rapurapu, Omahine, and Waiomou Roads, reached from either the Hamilton–Tauranga or Hamilton–Rotorua highways.

Ohinemuri River

The Ohinemuri River rises in the ranges behind Whangamata and flows west through the rugged Karangahake Gorge parallel to the Paeroa–Waihi highway. There is excellent fishing throughout the Ohinemuri, especially upstream of Waihi and through the Karangahake Gorge, where there is a variety of fishing water. About equal numbers of rainbow and brown trout are present.

GUIDES AND CHARTERS

Peter Francis
15 Sandringham Road
Kingsland
09 846 5901
peter@fishing.net.nz

Neptune Fishing Charters
BBYC Marina
Half Moon Bay
Pakuranga
09 577 4031
fish from the 12 m MV Chantelle

Rakoa Charters
2 Pier
Westhaven Marina
Auckland
09 624 6171
cruise and fish the Hauraki Gulf

Ardmore Helicopters
Ardmore Airfield
Papakura
Auckland
09 298 1899
info@chopper.co.nz
www.chopper.co.nz
fly to land-based fishing adventures

Waitawheta River

A boulder stream which flows through forest and farmland catchments before joining the Ohinemuri River. Highly valued for its scenic beauty and solitude. Access to the lower reaches is gained by crossing the Ohinemuri River at Karangahake township; the middle and upper reaches by taking the Waitawheta Road near Waikino on the Waihi–Paeroa highway, then either Dickey Flat, Dean or Franklin Roads. From the Dickey Flat and Franklin Roads there are Department of Conservation tracks along the river giving access to many kilometres of fishing water through scenic kauri forests.

Waimakariri Stream

The Waimakariri is a large spring-fed stream which flows north from the Kaimai Ranges to meet the Waihou River just south of the Okoroire Falls. This river is renowned for its high catch-rate of smallish trout; however, larger trout are present, especially in the upper reaches. Probably one of the best dry fly streams in the region. Access is off the Tirau–Rotorua highway and Waimakariri Road.

GUIDES AND CHARTERS

Water-rat
Half Moon Bay
Pakuranga
021 394 403
waterratfishing@bigfoot.com
www.waterrat.co.nz
saltwater fly fishing in the Hauraki Gulf

Anglers Lodge
1446 Colville Road
Amodeo Bay
North Coromandel
07 866 8584
anglers@clear.net.nz
www.anglers.co.nz
fishing charters to snapper-rich Coromandel waters

Matarangi Charters
Kenwood Drive
Matarangi
Whitianga
07 866 2498
fishing out of Matarangi

Scott Hollis-Johns
PO Box 654
Tauranga
07 543 0555
fishart@xtra.co.nz
fresh and salt water fly fishing in the Bay of plenty

Don Bryant
Minerva II
Panera Street
Kawhia
07 871 0848
west coast fishing out of Kawhia

WHANGANUI RIVER SYSTEM

Whanganui River

Between Taumarunui and Kakahi there are many good fishing pools. Access is from Taumarunui, or via the villages of Mahoe (Mahoe Road), Piriaka (from the power

29

station), Manunui (Mahoe Road), and Kakahi (Ako Street), and from the end of Te Rena Road by crossing the Whakapapa River and taking the short path across the Whakapapa Island. Access to the upper reaches within the Tongariro National Park is via old logging roads from State Highway 47 – a good topographical map or local knowledge is required.

Whakapapa River

One of New Zealand's finest trout fisheries but certainly not for the faint-hearted, as the Whakapapa alternates between turbulent rapids, deep pools and long boulder runs. The lower sections can be reached from the end of Te Rena Road via the village of Kakahi. The middle reaches are accessed from Owhango, south of Taumarunui, where a good gravel road leads to a bridge across the river. Just before the bridge, a short road on the right leads to a fenceline along which a path gives excellent access to the river. To get to the upper reaches you need to cross private farmland or follow the Tongariro Power Scheme intake structure off State Highway 47.

Ongarue River

A large tributary of the Whanganui offering many kilometres of fishing water and some of the best fishing in the district. It is mainly fished in its upper reaches above the township of Waimiha. Access is from the Ongarue Stream Road across private farmland. Below Waimiha there is some excellent spin fishing water, with access from the Waimiha–Ongarue Road, which runs parallel to the river.

Waimiha Stream

A delightful stream offering a succession of long ripples and pools containing a good population of both rainbow and brown trout. The lower and middle reaches offer clear, low banks providing relatively easy fishing. Access is from Waimiha Valley Road, which runs parallel with the stream, across private farmland – permission is required from the farmhouse just north of the Waimiha–Ongarue Road turn-off. Access can also be obtained across farmland from Ongarue Stream Road. The upper reaches of Waimiha run parallel to State Highway 30 (Te Kuiti–Mangakino), east of Bennydale, with access across private farmland. Regarded as a fly fisher's dream.

HANG YOUR HOOK

Malolo House
110 Commercial Road
Helensville
09 420 7262
maolo@xtra.co.nz
restored kauri villa close to Lake Ototoa

Buffalo Lodge
Buffalo Road
Coromandel
07 866 8960
buffalo@wave.co.nz
www.buffalolodge.co.nz
bush retreat with sweeping views

Park House
70 Queen Street
Cambridge
07 827 6368
park.house@xtra.co.nz
designed in 1920 as a private inn in Georgian style

Souter House
19 Victoria Street
Cambridge
07 827 3610
souter.house@xtra.co.nz
restored Victorian home built in 1875 and furnished with fine antiques

Tapanui
1714 Oparure Road
RD5 Te Kuiti
07 877 8549
tapanui@xtra.co.nz
magnificent farmstay-style lodge in spacious rural setting, close to Waitomo Caves

Out in the Styx
2117 Arapununi Road
Pukeatua,
RD1 Te Awamutu
07 872 4505
a rural bed and breakfast retreat in the heart of the Waikato

Waipari Lodge
PO Box 440
Taumarunui
07 896 6084
puketapu3a@xtra.co.nz
rustic lodge in central North Island wilderness

Waitomo Colonial Motel
58–59 Main North Road
Otorohanga
07 873 8289
oto@xtra.co.nz
within easy reach of Waitomo Caves and a range of trout streams

Anglers Lodge Motel
1446 Colville Road
Amodeo Bay
North Coromandel
07 866 8584
anglers@clear.net.nz
nestled in a sheltered valley bounded by a clear bush stream

Puka Park Resort
Mount Avenue
Pauanui
0800 785 272
pukaparkresort@xtra.co.nz
panoramic mountain and ocean views from the peace of private chalets

Villa Toscana Lodge
Ohuka Park
PO Box 43
Whitianga
(07) 866 2293
giorgio@villatoscona.co.nz
www.villatoscana.co.nz
a true Tuscan villa nestled amongst native bush high above Mercury Bay on the Coromandel Peninsula

MAROKOPA RIVER SYSTEM

Marokopa River

The Marokopa is a relatively remote west coast river that flows through some of the most beautiful bush scenery in the country. The river is divided into two fisheries by the impressive Marokopa Falls. Below the falls there is about 3 km of fishing probably best suited for spin fishing. Above the falls there is about 10 km of productive water. Both rainbow and brown trout are present. Access is from Te Anga Road, via Waitomo Caves Road.

Tawarau River

The Tawarau River enters the Marokopa River just below the Marokopa Falls. This river is remote, with foot access only to the upper and middle reaches. The scenery is very impressive as the river flows past high limestone cliffs and dense forests. There is a good track alongside the river which leads

CATCH A MEAL

Doyle's Licensed Seaside Restaurant
21 The Esplanade
Whitianga
07 866 5209
fresh local fare prepared in a creative way

Roselands
Fullerton Road
Waitomo Caves
07 878 7611
roselands@xtra.co.nz
award winning restaurant in a rural landscape

Kaiaua Seafood Restaurant
Coast Road
Kaiaua
09 232 2776
regularly judged the best fish and chips in the country

Grandpa Thorns Log Cabin Restaurant
4 Waitete Road
Waihi
07 863 8708
a_Berwick@xtra.co.nz
seafood and game

On the Rocks Bar and Restaurant
20 The Esplanade
Whitianga
07 866 4833
dunnland@ontherocks.co.nz
www.ontherocks.co.nz
seafood and venison

The Hunting Lodge
8259 Waikoukou Valley Rd
Waimauku
09 411 8259
www.thehuntinglodge.co.nz
much-loved country restaurant

to the Mangaohae Stream, and several suitable camping sites for a weekend trip. Access to the north end of the track is by Speedies Road via the Te Anga Road (Marokopa–Waitomo Caves).

COROMANDEL RIVERS

Kauaeranga River
This river flows westward along the Kauaeranga Valley before entering the sea at Thames. It offers over 20 km of good fishing, wadeable over a shingle and boulder bottom. Access is off Kauaeranga Valley Road behind Thames.

Waiwawa River
Rainbow trout are present in all rivers and streams that enter Whitianga Harbour. The Waiwawa is probably the best of these waters, a superb small-trout river with over 10 km of fishable water. Access is off the Coroglen–Tapu Road. The Mahakirau River is also popular with local anglers.

AUCKLAND WATERS

Lake Ototoa
Near Helensville on the South Kaipara Heads, this lake provides excellent fishing in very clear water. The successful introduction of the dwarf inanga as a food source has produced some excellent trout, with catches of up to 3 kg reported. The lake is on Donohue Road, off South Head Road.

Lake Whatihua (Thomsons)
A small lake beside the Waiuku–Kariotahi Road about 1.5 km from Kariotahi Beach. It is fishable around the shore, with excellent rises on calm days and in the evenings, but permission is required from the local landowner.

Lake Otamatearoa (Muirs)
Stocked with both rainbow and brown trout, a small boat is required for fishing, but access – off Whiriwhiri Road via the Waiuku–Otaua Road – is

33

good. The Waiuku race-track circles the lake. Permission is required from the landowner – the house just north of the lake.

Parkinsons Lake

Another small lake off Whiriwhiri Road, but it holds some good-sized rainbows. Easily wadeable but weed can be a problem.

Lake Tomarata

A small scenic lake about 20 km north of Wellsford. Regularly stocked with rainbow trout. An absence of weeds makes it pleasant for the shore-based angler.

Mangatangi Reservoir

This large water reservoir holds both wild and stocked rainbow trout. At present access for anglers is restricted to the dam wall, but limited boat access is available to members of the Auckland Freshwater Anglers Club. Access is from State Highway 2 (Auckland–Thames) and then Mangatangi, Kaiaua and Workman Roads.

Mangatawhiri Reservoir

A large water reservoir holding wild rainbow trout. At present, access for anglers is restricted to the dam wall. Access is via the village of Hunua, then south on Hunua Road, and then Moumoukai Road.

Lake Pupuke

In the heart of North Shore City, Lake Pupuke is regularly stocked with rainbow trout. Popular fishing locations include Sylvan Park and the end of Northcote Road.

Wairoa River

The closest river to Auckland City – offering 5 km of fishing water over wadeable shingle bed. Access is off McNicol Road via the Clevedon–Kawakawa Road. A fledgling wild fishery that the volunteers from Trout Unlimited are making better every year.

WHEN THE FISH DON'T BITE

Tasman Rides
Fordyce Road
Helensville
09 420 8603
025 864 093
info@tasmanrides.co.nz
www.tasmanrides.co.nz
farm, forest and beach on horseback

Kiwi Dundee Adventures
PO Box 198
Whangamata
07 865 8809
kiwi.dundee@xtra.co.nz
www.kiwidundee.co.nz
personalised hikes to historic reaches of the Coromandel

Matatoki Farm Cheese
State Highway 26
12 km south of Thames
07 868 1284
sample award-winning cheeses

Castle Rock Winery
State Highway 25
Te Rerenga
Coromandel
07 866 4542
sample fruit and vegetable wine produced from organically-grown local produce

Driving Creek Railway
Driving Creek Road
Coromandel
07 966 9703
www.drivingcreekrailway.co.nz
ride a narrow-gauge mountain railway to Barry Brickell's renowned pottery

Matarangi Golf Links
Matarangi Drive
Matarangi
07 866 5394
Bob Charles-designed links course

Black Water Rafting
Black Water Café
State Highway 37
Waitomo
07 878 6219
0800 228 464
bwr@blackwaterrafting.co.nz
www.blackwaterrafting.co.nz
glow-worms and underground rafting – with hot showers to follow

Canyonz
PO Box 68057
Newton
Auckland
09 357 0133
info@canyonz.co.nz
abseil, swim, slide and jump down a secret Waitakere Ranges stream

Waitomo Glow-worm Caves
Waitomo Caves Road
Waitomo
07 878 8227
info@waitomocaves.co.nz
www.waitomocaves.co.nz
glide through the glittering glow-worm grotto

MV *Waipa Delta*
Memorial Park Jetty
Memorial Drive
Hamilton
waipadelta@xtra.co.nz
www.waipadelta.co.nz
dinner cruise on New Zealand's longest river

Goldfields Railway
Waihi Station
Wrigley Street
Waihi
07 863 8251
ride a vintage steam train through the Karangahake Gorge

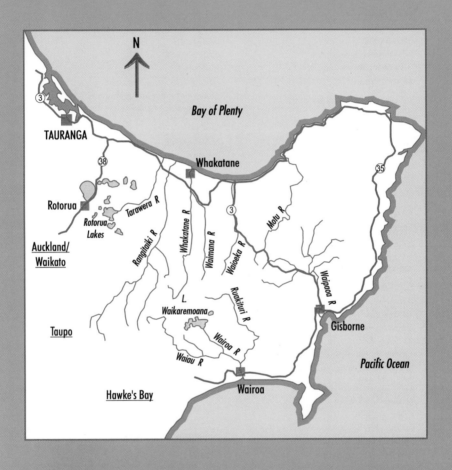

N

Bay of Plenty

TAURANGA

Whakatane

Rotorua

Tarawera R

Rotorua Lakes

Auckland/ Waikato

Rangitaiki R

Whakatane R

Waimana R

Waioeka R

Motu R

Waipaoa R

Gisborne

Taupo

L. Waikaremoana

Ruakituri R

Wairoa R

Waiau R

Pacific Ocean

Hawke's Bay

Wairoa

Eastern

The Eastern region is possibly the most diverse trout fishery in New Zealand. With the exception of alpine high-country streams, there is not a trout habitat that you cannot find in this huge region which covers almost a quarter of the North Island.

The chain of Rotorua lakes lie pretty much at the centre of the region and are mostly responsible for its reputation as a productive trout fishery. The lakes are regularly stocked with hatchery-reared fish, as well as from wild spawning in tributary streams, and fish numbers are always good. Most lake fish are taken trolling but there are also extensive opportunities for shoreline fly fishing.

What sets Rotorua lakes fishery apart, however, is Rotorua itself. As the North Island's most popular tourist area, there is no shortage of places to stay and things to do between casting a fly. That makes Rotorua an ideal destination for couples or families where not everyone is an ardent fisher. As well, trolling along the shoreline on almost any one of Rotorua's 13 fishable lakes is an effortless, and mostly productive, fishing option for novice trout fishers.

Spreading out from Rotorua, rather like the spokes on a bicycle wheel, is a vast network of rivers, streams, hydro lakes and wilderness fishing areas. There is world-renowned wilderness fishing in rivers such as the Ruakituri, Motu and Waioweka. These are paradise settings for fishers who prefer to stalk trout in the solitude of the back country. The Rangitaiki and Waikato rivers are

FAMOUS FOR	
• Hot pools and bubbling mud	• Te Urewera National Park
• The world's largest plantation pine forest	• Rotorua Marathon
• Big game fishing	• East Cape
	• Kiwifruit

generally more open rivers, while Te Urewera National Park in the east of the region encompasses some exciting wilderness fishing in both lakes and rivers.

In the summer there is some exceptional fishing on Lake Waikaremoana as big browns cruise the lake shore shallows for terrestrial insects. Hydro lakes on the Waikato River and at Aniwhenua are also productive. The 250 ha of Lake Aniwhenua was created in the late 1970s by the damming of the Rangitaiki River. There was an instant richness of food which produced some huge trophy fish, both rainbow and brown. While that first flush has gone, Aniwhenua remains a big fish lake.

INFORMATION

Fish and Game New Zealand Eastern Region
Paradise Valley Road
Private Bag 3010
Rotorua
07 357 5501
07 357 5503 (fax)

Gisborne office:
06 867 0390
www.fishandgame.org.nz

Regional Manager: Steve Smith
021 888 669
Senior Fisheries Officer: Rob Pitkethley
025 245 6328

Tourism Eastland
209 Grey Street
Gisborne
06 868 6139
info@gisborne.com
www.gisbornenz.com

Opotiki Visitor Information Centre
cnr St John and Elliott Streets
Opotiki
07 315 8484
InfoCentre@xtra.co.nz

Whakatane Visitor Information Centre
Boon Street
Whakatane
07 308 6058
whakataneinfo@xtra.co.nz

Tauranga Visitor Information Centre
95 Willow Street
Tauranga
07 578 8103
www.nztauranga.com

Tourism Rotorua
67 Fenton Street
Rotorua
07 348 5179
www.rotoruanz.com

WHERE AND WHAT

The Eastern Fish and Game region runs from Wairoa in the south, across to the Rangitaiki River headwaters and up through Huka Falls and Lake Maraetai, then along the Kaimai ranges to Tauranga Harbour.

There is a vast range of options; wilderness fishing in the Te Urewera National Park in the east and on rivers such as the Ruakituri; a web of river fisheries in the Bay of Plenty; and some 13 fishable lakes in the Rotorua district.

Eastern Fish and Game has built a network of angler access tracks on the more popular waterways such as the Ngongotaha Stream in Rotorua and in the Rangitaiki catchment.

As well, the region has produced a series of detailed maps and guides that pinpoint specific fishing spots and outline the fishing regulations. The brochures are available free from Eastern Fish and Game or tackle shops.

The Eastern fishing regulations follow the general North Island regulations. Most lakes and rivers are open year-round, with the exception of some spawning beaches and streams. Lakes Tarawera, Rotoiti and Okataina are closed to fishing from 30 June to 1 October along some stretches of shoreline.

Downriggers, paravanes, weights to assist sinking of trolled lures and metal cored or wire lines are prohibited in Lakes Waikaremoana and Waikareiti. Several waters are restricted to fly fishing only – the Ohau Channel, the Waiteti, Awahou and Hamurana streams and mouths; the Utuhina Stream above the Devon Street bridge and the Ngongotaha Stream above the SH5 bridge; the stream mouths at Te Wairoa, The Landing, Waitangi Stream, Tarawera Outlet, Wairua Stream and Twin Creeks on Lake Tarawera; the Hopuruahine and Mokau Streams and their mouths on Lake Waikaremoana; the Aniwaniwa and Korokoro streams above the Aniwaniwa and Korokoro Falls; the Ngawhakairara Stream mouth in Lake Waikareiti; the Tarawera River from Lake Tarawera to the Tarawera Falls; the stream mouths at Tapuaekura (Coles) Bay, and Hauparu Bay on Lake Rotoiti from 1 April to 30 June; the stream mouths at Ruato Bay, Waiiti Stream and the Pipe at Northern Hinehopu on Lake Rotoiti from 1 April to 30 September; the stream mouths at the Log Pool and Rayners One and Rayners Two streams on Lake Okataina from 1 April to 30 June; the Horomanga, Wharekopae, Waioeka, Ruakituri and Hangaroa rivers; and Lakes Whakamarino and Kaitawa.

➤ There is no bag limit on the Waikato River and Waikato hydro lakes upstream from Maraetai Dam.

➤ On the Rotorua lakes and Lakes Waikaremoana and Waikareiti the daily limit is eight trout, at least 35 cm in length. On all other waters the daily limit is two trout, no minimum size.

➤ The daily bag limit on Lake Waikaremoana and Lake Rotorua and its tributaries for brown trout is two.

➤ Trout taken on the Ruakituri River must be no more than 60cm long; on Lake Tarawera and the Tarawera River above the falls, it is illegal to keep or kill any rainbow over 65cm.

➤ Fishing is prohibited between midnight and 5 am.

Casting 🎣 around

ROTORUA LAKES

There 10 fishable lakes within a 30 km radius of Rotorua city: Rotorua, Tarawera, Okataina, Rotoiti, Rotoma, Rotoehu, Rerewhakaaitu, Rotomahana, Okareka and Tikitapu (Blue Lake.) The Rotorua lakes are regularly stocked by releases of hatchery-reared trout.

Lake Rotorua

This is the Eastern region's biggest lake and also its major fish producer. Fish average from 1–1.5 kg but catches up to 3 kg are taken regularly. The lake holds both brown and rainbow trout but the rainbows predominate. There is safe wading at all stream mouths where trout tend to congregate from December to the end of February, providing excellent fly fishing. However, shallow trolling using fly lines and streamer flies tends to be the most popular – and productive – fishing method, particularly from late March when water in the shallow lake has cooled and trout have dispersed.

Ngongotaha Stream

The Ngongotaha Stream is the most noted trout stream to empty into Lake Rotorua and is the lake's main spawning stream. The upper reaches are for fly fishing only but spinning is permitted below the State Highway. The mouth of the stream fishes well at most times of the year and the upper reaches are good nymphing waters during the season. Large areas of land adjacent to the Ngongotaha Stream are privately owned and anglers should only use the signposted access points.

Waiteti Stream

The Waiteti promises excellent fishing throughout the year downstream from the Ngongotaha Road bridge. There is good signposted access along the Rotorua District Council reserves on the true right of the stream. Above the Ngongotaha Road bridge access is limited and there is a closed season. Some excellent browns have been taken from the Waiteti.

Awahou Stream and Hamurana Stream mouths

Both stream mouths offer great summer fly fishing. The streams are open below the Hamurana Road bridges all year round. Wet fly fishing in the lower streams and off the rip at Hamurana during the summer is recommended. Access to the Awahou is just past Taniwha Springs. This is a Maori village and the residents' property – traditional rights and surroundings must be respected. Undisturbed water in early morning can be very good to the wading angler but in general most fishing is done from late afternoon onwards. Night fishing is usually excellent at both stream mouths.

Lake Tarawera

Tarawera – a deep, clear lake – is renowned as being the home of a strain of huge fish developed by Dr Peter Mylechreest, a scientist with the Eastern Fish and Game Council. The Tarawera Selective Breeding Programme he initiated liberates slower-maturing fish that have fast growth rates during the immature stage. Many fish in excess of 4 kg are caught every year. It is illegal to keep wild trout over 65 cm in length caught from Lake Tarawera. If the fish is over 65 cm and doesn't have a fin clip or tag, release it carefully back into the water alive so it can be used to produce good numbers of big hatchery fish in years to come.

Tarawera is reached after an attractive drive past the Blue and Green Lakes after turning right at Ngapuna on SH30 to Whakatane Highway. Boats can be launched at the Landing and Boat Shed Bay. Deep trolling produces great fish throughout the season, especially in the summer when fish move into the deeper waters. Harling a fly over shelves and drop-offs is often productive early in the season. Fly fishing is more successful after late March, both wading and from anchored boats. Rangiuru Bay and the Tarawera Landing are recommended night-time fly areas.

Lake Okataina

Considered the brightest jewel in the crown of Rotorua lakes, Okataina is completely surrounded by a scenic reserve which makes the fishing among the most scenically delightful you'll find anywhere and as close to wilderness fishing as most lakes can get. It is also a 'big trout' lake that has benefited from the Tarawera Selective Breeding Programme. The lake, 10 km from

Rotorua and separated from Tarawera by a narrow strip of land, has only one access road. The fishing is mainly by trolling. Fly fishing from a boat is popular at most stream mouths such as the Log Pool and Rayners One and Two. Shoreline fly fishing at the main beach and the rocky points either side often catches trophy fish in the winter months.

Lake Rotoiti and the Ohau Channel

Rotoiti is connected to Lake Rotorua by the Ohau Channel and holds both rainbow and brown trout. Rotoiti trout use the channel to reach spawning streams in Lake Rotorua so the channel provides productive river-style fly fishing early and late in the season when the fish are on the move. Lake Rotoiti is deep and fishing is mainly by trolling but there is renowned night fishing off the beach at Ruato Bay and the Waiiti stream mouth on the highway to Whakatane. Access to the Waiiti, the largest stream flowing into Rotoiti, is a little distance on the Rotorua side of the stream.

GUIDES AND CHARTERS

Bryan Colman
32 Kiwi Street
Rotorua
07 348 7766
bcolman@wave.co.nz
www.troutfishingrotorua.com

Clearwater Charters
537 Spencer Road
Lake Tarawera
RD5 Rotorua
07 362 8590

Crosscat Charters
Tauranga Marina
Tauranga
07 544 2374
fish the rich waters of the Bay of Plenty from the MV Catalyst

Clark Gregor
33 Haumoana Street
Rotorua
07 347 1123
fish@troutnz.co.nz

Greg Tuuta
State Highway 30
Lake Rotoiti
Rotorua
07 362 7794
greg@ikanuicharters.com

Frank Murphy
PO Box 16
Motu
Gisborne
06 863 5822
murphy.motu@xtra.co.nz

Rick Pollock
62 Arawa Road
Whakatane
07 308 5442

Graeme Ryder
Lake Aniwhenua Lodge
Galatea Road
RD1 Murupara
07 366 4777
trout.guide@xtra.co.nz
www.troutguides.co.nz

D.W. & R.N. Ward
6 Manuariki Ave
Ngongotaha
Rotorua
07 357 4974

Lake Rotoma and Lake Rotoehu

Two shallow and weed-prone lakes virtually side by side where the fishing is almost exclusively by trolling along the edge of the weed beds. Shoreline fishing is possible – although difficult – from some beaches and rocky points. The lakes seem to be dependent on artesian supply and underground drainage. A few inlets that are little more than drains are productive at night but they are difficult to find and even harder to get to.

Lake Rerewhakaaitu and Lake Rotomahana

Rerewhakaaitu is a relatively shallow lake accessed off SH38 and is one of the better Rotorua lakes for shore-based fishing. It also has good shoreline access, with the best boat-ramp in the Homestead arm off Brett Road, and is favoured by mobile-home owners because there is free camping available at a lakeside reserve. As with all lakes, trolling or harling along the weed beds with a sinking fly line is also popular and productive. Rotomahana is one of the least fished lakes, probably because a boat is virtually essential and as the lake is a bird sanctuary, motors are banned during May. However, those prepared to put in the effort usually enjoy good rewards.

Lake Okareka

Only 10 minutes' drive from the centre of Rotorua, Lake Okareka offers good fly fishing at the stream at Boyes Beach and the ski club in autumn.

Lake Tikitapu (Blue Lake)

Lake Tikitapu has an all-weather boat-ramp at the main beach. Harling and shoreline fishing are the most productive. Lake Tikitapu also contains a remnant stock of brook trout so keep an eye out for these attractive fish.

THE BAY OF PLENTY

The Bay of Plenty offers a variety of angling experiences, from small lake fisheries to scenic headwater fisheries within National Parks. A number of pamphlets are available on specific catchments within the bay and a general outline from west to east follows.

Wairoa River

The Wairoa below McLarens Falls has both brown and rainbow trout and spinning is the most productive way to take fish. Be aware of water level changes when the rafting days are on as flows can increase dramatically. The Wairoa has several tributaries where some surprisingly large fish hide out in the pools.

Ngamuwahine River

The Ngamuwahine is one of the more scenic rivers in the area and holds good numbers of brown trout up to 3 kg. Dry fly in the summer is one of the better ways to get the fish, and a spinner also works well. Access is off SH39 at Ngamuwahine Road. The road end leads to a walk into the Kaimai-Mamaku Forest Park and fishing is good both above and below the bushline.

Kaituna River

The Kaituna River flows from Lake Rotoiti to the sea at Maketu. The river holds good numbers of brown and rainbow trout and foot access is mainly through private property so landowner permission is required. The best access can be gained by boat from the ramp at the Maungarangi Road bridge off SH33.

Tarawera River

The Tarawera flows from Lake Tarawera through Kawerau to the sea at Matata. Exciting fishing exists in the forests above Kawerau and a Fletcher Challenge Forest access permit is required. The best access is from River Road and rainbow trout are present in high numbers in swift waters and average around 1.5 kg.

Whakatane River

The Whakatane River flows northwards from deep in the Te Urewera National Park at Ruatahuna to the coast at Whakatane. The river holds good populations of middle-sized brown and rainbow trout in a very scenic environment. The river is accessible from either end, with the headwaters reached from SH38 at Ruatahuna. The Ruatoki Valley Road off Reid Road at Taneatua follows the river upstream from the lower reaches to the Park boundary. Access from the road to the lower reaches is across private property so the landowners' permission is necessary. The middle reaches are accessed from a riverbank track that runs from the Ruatoki Road end through the National Park, joining the upper and lower road access points. Nymph and dry flies are the common mid-headwater lures and there are some good wet fly pools below the Park in the lower reaches.

TACKLE BOX

Hickeys Sportsworld
122 Church Street
Opotiki
06 315 6238
sportsworld.opotiki@xtra.co.nz

O'Keefe's Fishing Specialists
113 Eruera Street
Rotorua
07 346 0178

Broncos Sports World Ltd
Willow Street
Tauranga
07 578 6904

Hamills
1271 Fenton Street
Rotorua
07 343 3147

Fishermans Workshop
62 White Street
Rotorua
07 348 7156

Quality Bait & Tackle
10 Pohutu Street
Whakatane
07 308 7528

Port Rod & Reel
Fisherman's Wharf
Ohope
Whakatane
07 312 4318

Waimana River

The Waimana River is the main tributary of the Whakatane River. It holds good numbers of both brown and rainbow trout and has some of the most scenic fishing in the region. Access is good throughout its length. The middle to upper reaches are reached from SH2, turning off at Bell Road and continuing through Matahi Valley Road. Nymph fishing is the preferred method in the upper reaches. Late summer can often see a very good lace moth rise so dry flies should be carried at this time of year.

Waioeka River

The Waioeka River runs into the sea at Opotiki and is accessed along much of its length from SH2 between Opotiki and Gisborne. A full information pamphlet detailing this area is available. The catchment has a range of accessible areas and offers some picturesque fishing for good numbers of brown and rainbow trout in the 1–2 kg range.

RANGITAIKI CATCHMENT

The Rangitaiki River catchment is the largest in the Eastern Fish and Game region. It offers lake, small stream, and big river fishing opportunities. Angling information on this catchment is contained within the Rangitaiki pamphlet and is available throughout the region.

Rangitaiki River

The upper Rangitaiki River is within the Kaingaroa Forest and a Fletcher Challenge Forest access permit is required. The Otamatea and Dry Fly creeks can be accessed from Eastern Boundary Road and this also provides access to the upper river and Te Awa camping ground. The mid river and Waihua and Mangamako Streams can be accessed from Galatea Road off SH30.

Whirinaki River

The Whirinaki can be accessed from Ngatimanawa Road and the bridge on Whirinaki Road. There is a truck that runs alonside the river through most of this section. Access to higher reaches is via SH38, Okuia Road, Minginui Road and River Road. A number of signed access points run off all these roads and the river contains high densities of both brown and rainbow trout in a scenic bush setting.

Horomanga River

The Horomanga can be accessed from bridges on Galatea and Troutbeck Roads, and also from the Te Urewera National Park boundary at the end of the gravel road on the south side of the Troutbeck Road bridge. The Horomanga provide excellent late season wet fly and nymphing for spawning runs from Lake Aniwhenua.

Lake Aniwhenua

There is a boat-ramp and free camping area for Lake Aniwhenua at the end of Black Road. A track runs up the eastern side of the lake from this camping area. Small boats can also be launched at access points off Rabbit Bridge on Kopuriki Road. Aniwhenua provides good rainbow and brown trout to shoreline fly and spoon, or stalking fish from drifting boats. Trophy trout still exist here.

HANG YOUR HOOK

The Lake House
6 Cooper Ave
Holdens Bay
Rotorua
07 345 3313
susank@xtra.co.nz
*on the lake edge at Holdens Bay with views
over Lake Rotorua to Mokoia Island*

Motuhora Rise
2 Motuhora Rise
Whakatane
07 307 0224
jtspell@xtra.co.nz
*purpose-built B&B nestled in the hilltops
above Whakatane*

Trout Lodge
Gemini Place
Kawaha Point
Rotorua
07 349 1000
info@troutlodge.co.nz
*excellent fly-fishing all year round from the
front lawn*

Kawaha Point Lodge
171 Kawaha Point Road
Kawaha Point
Rotorua
07 346 3602
kawaha.lodge.rotorua@xtra.co.nz
*professional fishing guides will collect you
from a private jetty*

The Home of Hardy
104 Parawai Road
Ngongotaha
Rotorua
07 357 4743
base@hardy.co.nz
*lakefront lodge with two self-contained
cottages – private jetty*

Ariki Lodge
2 Manuariki Ave
Ngongotaha
Rotorua
07 357 5532
rgforgie@xtra.co.nz
*on the lake edge just a few metres from the
Ngongotaha stream*

Ngongotaha Lakeside Lodge
41 Operiana Street
Ngongotaha
Rotorua
07 357 4020
ktm@clear.net.nz
*trout fishing host who will share his
knowledge*

Waiteti Lakeside Lodge
2 Arnold Street
Ngongotaha
Rotorua
07 357 2311
*at the Waiteti Stream mouth with its own
boat-ramp and fishing guide host*

Riverview Cottage
State Highway 2
Waioeka Gorge
RD1 Opotiki
07 315 5553
riverview.cottage@xtra.co.nz
*colonial-style cottage on a farm site
overlooking the river*

Tunanui State Cottages
1001 Tunanui Road
Opoutama
Mahia
Tunanui@xtra.co.nz
cosy cottage on a 1200 ha sheep station

47

Flaxy Lakes and Canals

The Rangitaiki Canal is accessed off Kiorenui Road, and from the canal Bush Road runs up to Flaxy Lake and Flaxy Canal. This area provides very good summer fishing with fly and spoon to brown and rainbow trout.

TE UREWERA/EAST COAST

A number of spectacularly scenic and exciting fisheries are available on the eastern side of the region and the trip to the area is well worth it. Bush-clad lake and river fishing is the main feature in this area, along with a variety of opportunities to catch some large trout in special places.

Lake Waikaremoana

Lake Waikaremoana is made up of two distinct fisheries – the shoreline brown trout and the trolling rainbow trout fishery. Excellent fly fishing from the shore and the skill involved in stalking the large brown trout that cruise the shallows entice a number of anglers to the lake. The Waikaremoana fishery is covered in detail in its own Fish and Game information pamphlet which gives further insights into fishing methods and secluded spots. Lake Waikaremoana is a wild fishery but some tagged fish are liberated each year.

Brown and rainbow trout were liberated into Lake Waikaremoana in 1896. It is the largest lake in the Te Urewera National Park and is accessed off SH38. There are a number of access points and boat-ramps from turn-offs as the road winds around the side of the lake. Camping, excellent track and boat-ramp facilities make this part of Te Urewera National Park a must for anglers of all persuasions. Spinning from the shore may also be productive, as can harling a fly in shallow areas. Mid-October through until mid-June is recommended for fishing brown trout, which average 2 kg. Fish up to 4 kg are sometimes taken.

Rainbow trout are common in the deeper parts of Lake Waikaremoana. Again, they are of a good size, and may weigh more than 3 kg. Trolling is popular, particularly from Te Puna Bay to Waiopaoa Bay, or under the Panekiri bluffs. From Opourau Bay (Home Bay) to Te Whero Bay is another part of the lake recommended for trolling.

LAKE WAIKAREMOANA STREAMS

There are four major streams that feed into Lake Waikaremoana. Angling at the mouths provides exciting fishing from April as trout begin migrating upstream to spawn. The Hopuruahine and Mokau Stream mouths are the most popular. There are marker poles at the mouths of the major streams. Fly fishing only is permitted upstream from the marker poles.

Lake Waikareiti

Lake Waikareiti is reached by a walking track starting near the DoC Aniwaniwa Visitors Centre on SH38. The 45-minute walk to the lake is definitely worth the effort for the opportunity to fish in pristine surroundings and the rewarding wild rainbow trout that the lake offers. Trolling from dinghies or fly fishing from a drifting boat are the most popular methods. Summer months are the best time for shoreline fly fishing,

HANG YOUR HOOK

Acton Estate
577 Back Ormond Road
Gisborne
06 867 9999
restored Edwardian mansion in magnificent private setting

Lake Aniwhenua Lodge
Galatea Road
RD1 Murupara
07 366 4777
trout.guide@xtra.co.nz
www.troutguides.co.nz
trophy trout under professional guidance

Paparangi Ventures
PO Box 26
Motu
Gisborne
06 8635 882
www.paparangiventures.co.nz
wilderness retreat on the upper Motu River

Murphy's Lodge
PO Box 16
Motu
Gisborne
06 863 5822
murphy.motu@xtra.co.nz
easy walking distance to one of the world's classic dry fly rivers – the Motu – with classic New Zealand guide, Frank Murphy

Rangitaiki River Lodge
Golf Road
Murupara
Bay of Plenty
07 366 5507
info@flyfishinglodge.co.nz
www.flyfishinglodge.co.nz
spacious hotel-style lodge (will pick up guests from Rotorua Airport or Auckland Airport)

and Sandy Bay is an ideal location. Dinghies can be hired from the National Park headquarters at Aniwaniwa. There is a DoC hut at the lake for overnight stays.

Lake Whakamarino

Several fish of 4.5 kg and over are caught from Lake Whakamarino each season. The lake is also known as Tuai Lake, and is on SH38 just past Waikaremoana towards Wairoa. Very large trout, up to 12.5 kg, have earned this fishery its trophy reputation. Shoreline angling and fly fishing from an anchored boat are both popular. No motorised craft are allowed on the lake.

Lake Kaitawa

Motorised craft are not permitted on Lake Kaitawa, but it is possible to hand-launch dinghies. Casting a fly from an anchored boat is often successful, particularly from October to February.

Ruakituri River

The Ruakituri River is an internationally renowned fishery, holding good numbers of both brown and rainbow trout. A classic feature of Ruakituri fish is their extremely strong fighting abilities. Some very large fish are caught in this river each year and most average around 2–3 kg. General access to the lower and mid reaches of the river is from Ruakituri Road off SH36. Papuni Road also provides access to some higher mid reaches and the headwaters.

Upper Ruakituri River

The headwaters of the Ruakituri River lie above the Waitangi Falls, in Te Urewera National Park. Here anglers can

CATCH A MEAL

Trudy's Restaurant
Gisborne Hotel
cnr Huxley and Tyndall Streets
Gisborne
06 868 4109
renowned seafood chowder

Smash Palace Bar and Barbecue
Banks Street
Gisborne
06 867 7769
novel and legendary

Poppy's Villa
4 Marguerita Street
Rotorua
07 347 1700
excellent beef and lamb dishes

Timeout Tarawera
The Landing
Lake Tarawera
Rotorua
07 362 8595
overlooks the lake and Mt Tarawera

experience both spectacular scenery and a true wilderness fishing experience. The upper section of the river has a more rugged nature, but large boulders and open shallow channels make navigation easy for anglers. Only rainbow trout are present in this part of the river, but the upper Ruakituri River has earned a reputation as a pristine trophy fishery.

Anini Stream

Access to the Anini Stream is via Rua's Track through the Ruakituri Reserve on the true right of the river. The stream is made up of a bouldery streambed with bush-clad banks. Clear water and lots of cover mean that excellent trout habitat is present. Beautiful scenery is an added bonus for anglers. Deep shady pools upstream from the confluence are most likely to produce good results.

CATCH A MEAL

Sirocco
1280 Eruera Street
Rotorua
07 347 3388
Mediterranean cuisine

The Wharf Shed Bar and Brasserie
The Strand
Whakatane
07 308 5698
famous seafood chowder

Barnacles
122 The Strand
Whakatane
07 308 7429
seafood and takeaways

Harbourside Brasserie
62 The Strand East
Whakatane
07 308 6721
licenced steak-house

Waiau River

The Waiau River drains out of the south-eastern corner of Te Urewera National Park and into the Wairoa system. The headwaters of the Waiau support healthy populations of both brown and rainbow trout with some very high catch rates of fish in the 1–2.5 kg range. The wilderness setting makes it a beautiful river to fish, and summer dry fly and nymph fishing can be very productive. The lower river is accessed from SH38 and spinning is the best method. The middle reaches are reached from Putere Road off SH2 and again spinning and wet fly are best. The upper reaches are the real gem although access is difficult, via either long tramps from the Te Urewera National Park end (SH38) or Maungataniwha.

WHEN THE FISH DON'T BITE

White Island Tours
15 The Strand East
Whakatane
07 308 9500
www.whiteisland.co.nz
walk through an active volcano

Wet 'n' Wild Rafting
PO Box 601
Rotorua
07 348 34191
wetnwild@wave.co.nz
www.wetnwildrafting.co.nz
raft the Motu, Wairoa and Kaituna Rivers

Waimoana Horse Treks
Waimoana Station
End of Lysnar Street
Wainui Beach
Gisborne
06 868 8218
waimoana@ihug.co.nz
gallop along an ocean beach

Buried Village
Tarawera Road
RD5 Rotorua
07 362 8287
discover@buriedvillage.co.nz
the village of Te Wairoa buried by the eruption of Mt Tarawera in 1886

Rainbow Springs Trout and Wildlife Sanctuary
Ngongotaha
Rotorua
ogle at the trout you are not allowed to catch

Whakarewarewa Thermal Village Tours
Tryon Street
Whakarewarewa
Rotorua
07 349 3463
info@whakarewarewa.co.nz
Pohutu geyser, boiling mudpools and a hangi

Volcanic Wunderflites
Rotorua Airport
Te Ngae Road
Rotorua
07 345 6077
wunderflites@xtra.co.nz
www.eclipz.co.nz
volcanoes from a safe distance

Skyline Gondola, Restaurant and Luge
Fairy Springs Road
Rotorua
07 347 0027
enquiries@skylineskyrides.co.nz
www.skylinerides.co.nz
ride to a great view of Rotorua and fun on the luge

Agrodome
Western Road
Rotorua
07 357 1050
info@agrodome.co.nz
www.agrodome.co.nz
agricultural theme park

Hawke's Bay

Hawke's Bay is renowned for its award-winning wines and horticulture. This Pacific coast region on the east of the North Island averages 2245 hours of sunshine a year and is blessed with dry summers, mild winters and low humidity. Grapes thrive in its diverse soils and the wines produced from them have acquired an international reputation.

But then the region has always been a place where crops grow well. Supermarkets throughout New Zealand and Australia are stocked with fruit and vegetables grown under the generous Hawke's Bay sun. What is perhaps less well known is that winding among the wineries and fields devoted to horticulture are silver streams and rivers, flowing out of a back-country wilderness and home to fine rainbow and brown trout.

The river and stream systems meander east into the Pacific Ocean from the high country of the Ruahine or Kaweka Ranges and spread out across the rolling Heretaunga and Ruatainiwha Plains. It is a diverse landscape and the

INFORMATION

Fish and Game Hawke's Bay Region
22 Burness Road
Greenmeadows
Napier
06 844 2460
06 844 2461 (fax)
www.fishandgame.org.nz
Regional Manager: Steve Smith
Fish and Game Officer: Iain Maxwell

Napier Freshwater Anglers
PO Box 69
Napier

Napier Visitor Information Centre
100 Marine Parade
06 834 1911
info@napiervic.co.nz

Tourism Hawkes Bay
06 834 1918
hbt@hawkesbaytourism.co.nz
www.hawkesbaytourism.co.nz
www.hawkesbaynz.com

Hastings District Anglers' Club
c/o B Cottington
402 Lascelles Street
Hastings

Special Publications
Trout in Hawke's Bay, Fish and Game New Zealand
$6.50 from local sports goods shops, or Fish and Game offices

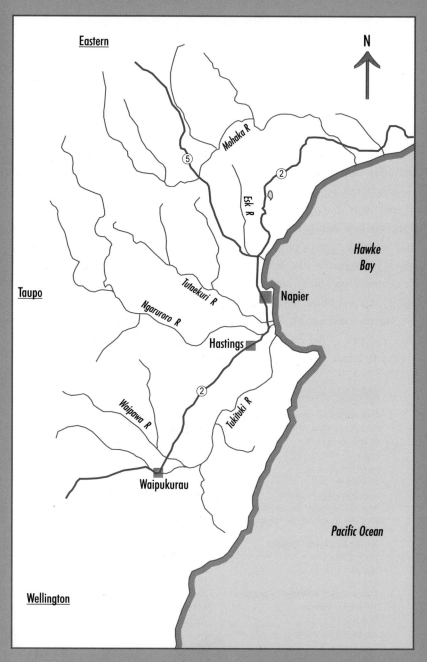

N

Eastern

Taupo

Mohaka R

Esk R

5

2

Tutaekuri R

Ngaruroro R

Napier

Hastings

2

Waipawa R

Tukituki R

Waipukurau

Wellington

Hawke Bay

Pacific Ocean

rivers such as the Mohaka, Ngaruroro, Tutaekuri, Waipawa and Tukituki, complement with superb trout-fishing prospects. The Mohaka River is the premier river, with recent Fish and Game dive surveys showing that it has one of the highest densities of trout in New Zealand, with up to 200 fish per kilometre in some sections.

Most of the 35 wineries in the region welcome visitors. So does Napier, the Art Deco capital of the world. The 1931 earthquake that destroyed much of the city and took 258 lives left an unusual legacy – rebuilding coincided with the Art Deco fashion of the times and now draws visitors from around the world, particularly during the annual Art Deco weekend every February. In keeping with its growing reputation as a tourist centre, Napier has turned its inner streets into delightful malls with outdoor cafés and a range of shops selling antiques and collectibles. If you are a collector of old fishing rods and reels, Napier and Hawke's Bay would be hard to beat for a most enjoyable trout-fishing weekend.

FAMOUS FOR

- Napier – Art Deco city
- Hawke's Bay wines
- Fruit and vegetables
- Ruahine Forest Park
- Cape Kidnappers gannet colony
- Te Aute College
- Te Mata Peak
- Marineland

WHERE AND WHAT

Fish and Game New Zealand's Hawke's Bay Region is bordered on the east by the Pacific Ocean, and encompasses the Mohaka River catchment in the north, down to the Tautane Stream in the south. The major river systems mostly rise in the west, running through either the Ruahine or Kaweka ranges before opening up onto the undulating country of the Heretaunga and Ruataniwha Plains and flowing into Hawke's Bay. Of these, the Mohaka, Ngaruroro, Tutaekuri, Waipawa and Tukituki are the most popular with anglers. Most fishing in the region is on rivers.

The Hawke's Bay fishing regulations follow the general North Island regulations. All lakes in the region are open year-round. Also open all year are the Tukituki River downstream from the SH50 road bridge; The Ngaruroro River downstream from its confluence with the Taruarau River; the Tutaekuri River downstream from its confluence with the Mangaone Stream; the Waipawa River downstream from the SH2 bridge; the Porangahau River downstream from its confluence with the Mangawhero Stream; the Karamu Stream; the Mohaka River downstream from the Mangatainoka River; the Waipunga River downstream from the falls. All other waters are closed to fishing from 30 April to 1 October.

There are no restrictions on the use of spinning tackle in any waters – but the Ngaruroro River above the Kiwi Creek junction, including its tributaries, is a designated catch and release water. Any trout caught must be released immediately with as little injury as possible.

Most rivers, streams and lakes in the region have a limit of two trout a day. There is no limit on Kuripapango, the larger of the two lakes known as the Twin Lakes.

On the Esk, Mohaka, and Ngaruroro Rivers between the Whanawhana cable and the Kiwi Creek junction, and including their tributaries, the daily limit is one fish. On the Mohaka River below the SH5 bridge, excluding tributaries, Blue Lake, Kuripapango West Lake, Opouahi Lake, Orakai Lake, Te Pohue Lake, Tutira and Waikopiro Lakes except Sandy Creek and Outlet Channel, the daily limit is four trout.

In most waters there is no minimum size, but in Lakes Tutira and Waikopiro the minimum takeable length is 35 cm. On the Esk River above the Ellis Wallace Road bridge, the Ngaruroro River above the Whanawhana cable, and the Taruarau River, and including their tributaries, trout that are taken must be no longer than 55 cm.

Fishing from motor-powered boats is prohibited on Lake Tutira and Lake Opouahi.

Casting around

MOHAKA RIVER AND SOME OF ITS TRIBUTARIES

This river runs from the Kaimanawa Forest Park to the sea, with endless kilometres of fishable water in between. Its bed has generally large boulders so care is needed when wading. The river holds both rainbow and brown trout, with rainbow generally predominating below Pakaututu Road and browns above that point. Fish are generally in excellent condition and some are very large.

Puketitiri Road, Pakaututu Road and Hot Springs Road give access to the upper reaches. The uppermost vehicular access is 'the gums' at the end of Hot Springs Road. Further downstream, the bridge over the Mohaka at Pakaututu Road is a popular entry point. The middle stretch of the river can be reached from Waitara Road and McVicars Road off the Napier–Taupo Highway at either sides of the Mohaka River bridge. The river can also be accessed in its middle reaches from Pohokura Road and Willow Flat Road. State Highway 2 gives access to the lower reaches.

All types of flies, nymphs and spoons are suitable for the Mohaka.

Ripia River

The Ripia is a tributary of the Mohaka which has its confluence just below the Pakaututu bridge on the Puketitiri Road. Both rainbow and brown trout are found – averaging 1 kg although there are larger fish present. The headwaters are difficult to reach but the river can be accessed from the junction at Pakaututu Road and fished upstream from there.

Te Hoe River

Both rainbow and brown trout are found weighing around 1–1.5 kg, but fish numbers are low. The river is reached off SH2 at the Tutira Store. Take the Pohokura Road to the bank of the Mohaka River opposite the Te Hoe junction. Permits to the upper river must be obtained from Carter Holt Forests, Napier (06 835 6390).

Waipunga River

A large portion of this tributary follows the Napier–Taupo Highway. The Waipunga holds both rainbow and brown trout of excellent quality, generally in the 1 kg upwards class. The river above the falls can be accessed via Pohokura Road. A permit is needed from the Fletcher Forests Visitor Centre, Rotorua (07 346 2082).

WAIKARI RIVER

The Waikari River at Putorino, a few kilometres north of Lake Tutira on SH2, holds well-conditioned rainbows of good size and fighting ability. Browns are found in the headwaters, which are reached from Heays Access Road. The river's upper reaches are easily accessed by turning right into Waikari Coast Road just past Putorino and then first left into Glenbrook Road.

LAKE OPOUAHI

This small lake is exceptionally clear and is situated in pleasant native surroundings near Tutira. It is best fished from a rowboat. The predominant species in Opouahi are brook trout (Savelinus fontinalis) but tiger and rainbow trout were also released for the first time in 1998.

LAKE TUTIRA AND LAKE WAIKOPIRO

This picturesque lake of around 178 ha has very easy access, is pleasant to fish and is generally productive. Hawke's Bay Fish and Game Council stocks the lake annually with rainbow and brown trout. Fish generally grow to a large size in the lake and a 5.2 kg brown was taken from Waikopiro in early July 1997.

There are now a number of tagged fish in the lake which can win those who return them to Fish and Game a free licence. The noxious weed *Hydrilla verticullata* is present in Tutira and no weed should be removed under any circumstances. Motorised boats are prohibited for this reason.

WAIKOAU RIVER AND AROPAOANUI RIVER

The Waikoau can be accessed from SH2 just north of the Devil's Elbow. The upper reaches can be accessed from Pohokura Road, off Matahoura Road, which turns left off SH2 at Tutira. Lower reaches can be fished via Aropaoanui Road which turns off SH2 at the summit of the Tongoia Hill before the Devil's Elbow.

ESK RIVER

Between Napier and Wairoa SH2 crosses the Esk River near its mouth just past the Napier–Taupo Highway (SH5) turn-off. The Ellis Wallace Road (turn right off the Napier–Taupo Highway just past Eskdale) follows the middle reaches for a considerable distance. The headwaters can

TACKLE BOX

Hamills
106 Nelson Street
Hastings
06 878 7177

Sportsworld Waipukurau
64 Ruataniwha Street
Waipukurau
06 858 9412

Pioneer Reel & Rifle
Main Road
Clive
Napier
06 870 0362

Tight Lines
89 Austin Street
Onekawa
Napier
06 843 6388

Guns and Tackle
44 Pandora Road
Ahuriri
Napier
06 835 9016

Wairo Motorcycles
cnr Mahia Ave and Carroll Street
Wairoa
06 838 6922

be accessed off Ohurakura Road, which turns off the Napier–Taupo Highway about 2 km before Te Pohue.

TUTAEKURI RIVER AND SOME OF ITS TRIBUTARIES

Mainly rainbow trout inhabit this river, although some browns are present too. Fish are in good condition, with an average weight around 1 kg in the lower reaches but with some much larger fish also available.

The upper river can generally be reached from various side roads off the Napier–Taihape Road. The middle reaches are most easily accessed from Puketapu and Dartmoor Roads to the west of Taradale. The lower reaches are accessed from behind Taradale township and there are numerous riverbank access points between there and the mouth. The major access points have been signposted by Fish and Game.

Mangaone River

This river has 32 km of fishable water and provides excellent fishing early in the season; however, weed growth during the summer months sometimes makes fishing difficult. Rainbow trout predominate but brown trout are also present. There are good-condition fish in the lower reaches, with an average weight of 1 kg but fish of 2.5 kg are not uncommon. The upper reaches contain generally smaller fish with excellent fighting ability.

GUIDES AND CHARTERS

David Dods
PO Box 38
Patutahi
Gisborne
06 862 7850

Simon Hustler
PO Box 2
Gisborne
06 862 4809

Robbie Greenslade
32 Rawiri Street
Gisborne
06 867 1214
greenslader@tangent.co.nz

Grant Petherick
805 Fitzroy Ave
Hastings
025 863 924
grantpetherick@xtra.co.nz
www.flyfishingwinetours.co.nz

Morris Hill
27 Tainui Drive
Havelock North
06 877 7642
troutfishing@jacktrout.co.nz
www.jacktrout.co.nz

NGARURORO RIVER AND SOME OF ITS TRIBUTARIES

This is a large, though wadeable river with over 100 km of fishable water. The lower and middle reaches usually fish well during the early months of the season with the middle and upper reaches giving better results later. Above the Napier–Taihape Road, the river gorges with deep sections and care should be taken. Rainbow trout predominate. Average weight is around 1 kg but many larger and heavier fish are taken throughout the season.

The middle and lower reaches are easily accessed with plenty of public roads crossing it at various points. The upper reaches offer excellent wilderness fishing for those prepared to walk in from Kuripapango or fly in to one of the many huts.

Taruarau River

This tributary joins the Ngaruroro some 10–15km below the Napier–Taihape Road. Its smaller size means it is an easy river to fish, and it is particularly good in the early season and over the summer months. It holds both rainbows and browns which average around 1 kg and are of excellent fighting quality. Access is from the Napier–Taihape Road over the Gentle Annie hill, about one and a half hours' drive from Napier.

Ohara Stream

This fairly large tributary fishes well in the early summer months. A cautious approach is required as the water is often clear and shallow. Fish often hold under eroded papa banks or deep in the heads of the pools. Only rainbow trout are present in this river. The average weight is around 1 kg, but larger fish are often taken.

Western Lake, Kuripapango

This small lake is worth a visit if you are in the Kuripapango Area, perhaps fishing the Ngaruroro. It has a large population of brown trout, generally of a smaller size.

HANG YOUR HOOK

Hawthorne Country House
420 State Highway 2
Pakipaki
Hastings
06 878 0035
hawthorne@xtra.co.nz
www.hawthorne.co.nz
tourism award-winning tranquillity in a rural setting

Tukipo Terraces
PO Box 114
Takapau
Hawke's Bay
06 855 6827
boutique lodging on a working deer farm

Cornucopia Lodge
361–363 State Highway 5
Eskdale
Napier
06 836 6508
info@cornucopia-lodge.com
www.cornucopia-lodge.com
close to Hawke's Bay wineries

Eskview Heights
261 Hill Road
Bayview
Napier
06 836 7190
eskviewheights@hotmail.com
semi-rural with panoramic views

Twinpeak
100 Puketapu Road
Taradale
Napier
06 844 9319
soe.twinpeak@xtra.co.nz
tranquil setting in the hills between Napier and Hastings

Mynthurst Farmstay
912 Lindsay Road
RD3 Waipukurau
Hawke's Bay
06 857 8093
mynthurst@xtra.co.nz
genuine farmstay on a 560 ha working cattle and sheep station

Silverford
358 Dartmoor Road
Puketapu
Napier
06 844 5600
homestay@iconz.co.nz
Tudor-style country residence set in 7 ha of garden

Mangapapa Lodge
466 Napier Road
Havelock North
Hawke's Bay
06 878 3234
elegant 19th-century mansion that was once the Wattie family home

The Greenhouse
288 Te Mata Road
Havelock North
Hawke's Bay
06 877 4904
the.greenhouse@xtra.co.nz
nestled in the corner of a vineyard among merlot and chardonnay grapes

Providencia
225 Middle Road
Havelock North
Hawke's Bay
06 877 2300
Queen Anne-style kauri villa with exquisite interior panelling and organic cuisine

CATCH A MEAL

Café Absolute
120 Taradale Road
Napier
06 843 4322
award-winning atmosphere

Peak House Restaurant
Te Mata Peak
Havelock North
06 866 8663
peak@clear.net.nz
fine food, unequalled view

Alfresco's Café & Bar
65 Emerson Street
Napier
06 835 1181
great food, great atmosphere

Ashes Restaurant
Heretaunga Park Motor Inn
826 Omahu Road
Hastings
06 876 6069
relaxed and comfortable atmosphere

Baggios
21 Hastings Street
Napier
06 834 0548
authentic Italian cuisine

The Stunned Mullet
209 Marine Parade
Napier
06 835 9188
seafood brasserie

Clive Grapery Restaurant
194 Main Road
Clive
Napier
06 870 0988
Mediterranean cuisine

Crown & Anchor Seafood Restaurant
Waghorne Street
Ahuriri
Napier
06 835 7999
seafood Napier-style

Hairy Cactus
39 Marine Parade
Napier
06 835 6626
Mexican-style

Mangapapa Lodge
Napier Road, RD2
Hastings
06 878 3234
classical cuisine in elegant surroundings

Marnies Restaurant
Hastings Street
Napier
06 835 3009
seafood, steak and pasta

Mombasa Restaurant
275 Gloucester Street
Taradale
Napier
06 844 2760
Mediterranean and New Zealand cuisine

Old Flame Restaurant
112 Tennyson Street
Napier
06 835 6848
stylish Art Deco surroundings

The Cat & Fiddle Ale House
502 Karamu Road North
Hastings
06 878 4111
Sunday roast in an English alehouse

TUKITUKI RIVER AND SOME OF ITS TRIBUTARIES

This is probably the best known river in the Hawke's Bay region, producing excellent fishing for both rainbow and brown. The river is 80 km long and generally fishable throughout its length. Fish of up to 4 kg have been common, however rainbows and brown trout of 1–2 kg predominate. The main river is detailed in a free brochure available from Fish and Game and tackle shops.

Tukipo River

This river holds good-condition fighting rainbows of around 1 kg. The upper reaches are accessed from SH50 which crosses it. The middle reaches can be accessed from Balfour Road, off SH50, and the lower reaches from the Ashcott–Waipukurau Road or from the Pukeora Bridge.

Waipawa River

This large tributary of the Tukituki flows alongside the township of the same name and its confluence with the Tukituki is just a few kilometres downstream from Waipawa. Both rainbow and brown trout are present at around 1 kg, but larger fish are regularly taken – large browns are common. Fish generally remain in good condition for most of the season.

The lower reaches can be accessed at various points around the Waipawa township and below. The middle reaches are accessed from Stockade Road, off Ongaonga Road, and the upper reaches

WHEN THE FISH DON'T BITE

Art Deco Napier
Tennyson Street
Napier
06 835 0022
artdeco@hb.co.nz
www.hb.co.nz/artdeco
shop@artdeconapier.com
www.artdeconapier.com
guided walks around the city

Gannet and Coastline Tours
0800 864 664
06 835 4446
info@gannet.co.nz
www.gannet.co.nz
visit the gannets at Cape Kidnappers

Balloon Flights
Napier
06 858 8480
www.early-am-balloons.co.nz
Hawke's Bay from an airborne basket

The Beach Drop
Marine Parade
Napier
0800 835 5184
www.napierskydive.co.nz
tandem skydiving

are available from Springhill and Makaroro Roads off SH50, and Caldwell Road off Wakarara Road.

Makaroro River

This large tributary of the Waipawa is an improving fishery well worth a visit. Both rainbow trout and brown trout are present, with best fishing early and late in the season. The junction with the Waipawa can be accessed by Makaroro Road, off SH50. The middle reaches can be accessed from Springhill Road, and the upper waters from Wakarara Mill Road.

Mangaonuku Stream

This stream is quite easily accessed from the Waipawa Road at the limeworks or Brow bridge. Rainbow trout predominate but brown trout are also present. Fish are generally in good condition and can reach 4 kg. Dry fly fishing with flies such as Brown Beetle, Red spinner and Black spinner early in the season provide excellent results.

WHEN THE FISH DON'T BITE

National Aquarium of New Zealand
Marine Parade
Napier
06 834 1404
info@nationalaquarium.co.nz
www.nationalaquarium.co.nz
experience another world without getting wet

Splash Planet
Grove Road
Hastings
06 876 9856
www.splashplanet.co.nz
take the kids for a ride

Vicky's Wine Tours
Napier
06 843 9991
gary.jo.newton@clear.net.nz
check out the Bay's famous wines

On Yer Bike
129 Rosser Road
RD4 Hastings
06 879 8735
info@onyerbike.net.nz
cycle tour to six wineries

MAREATOTARA STREAM

This stream is about 8 km from Havelock North on the Havelock–Waimarama Road. It is a challenging stream to fish due to its small size and generally clear water. Brown trout are released every year. Fish of 1.5 kg, and sometimes larger, of excellent condition and good eating quality, can be taken. The Havelock North–Waimarama Road gives access to much of this river. The upper and lower reaches are only accessed from private roads so landowner permission is required.

Above: Standing solidly on the shore of the Kerikeri Basin, Northland, since 1836 is the Stone Store.

Right: The 27 m-high Whangarei Falls carries the waters of the Waitaua and Mangakino Streams over the edge of an old basalt lava flow. Many Northland streams now hold self-sustaining wild trout.

Left: The Waihou River was the first in New Zealand to be stocked with rainbow trout and the upper reaches, fed by the crystal spring waters of Putaruru (Auckland/Waikato region), is still considered to be one of the country's best dry fly fisheries. Near Matamata the river is also fun for kayakers.

Below: The paddleboat MV *Waipa Delta* made its first run on the Waikato River in 1877. Now it is based in Hamilton and cruises the river while passengers sip afternoon tea or have a relaxing meal.

Right: New Zealand's longest river, the Waikato, flows through two Fish and Game regions and has been extensively modified by hydroelectric power schemes. But the river and its tributary streams still offer many opportunities for fly fishing and tramping.

Below: Nature's own fairy lights, the sparkling glow-worms that light up the Waitomo Caves (Auckland/ Waikato region), have been delighting tourists and locals alike since 1887.

TOURISM WAIKATO

TOURISM WAIKATO

Opposite Above: Winemakers have taken advantage of the sunny climate and alluvial soils of the Gisborne area in the Eastern region to produce some of the country's best chardonnays.

Opposite: Huge brown trout cruise the quiet shallows of Lake Waikaremoana (Hawke's Bay region).

Above: In the Eastern Bay of Plenty several rivers tumble out of the bushclad hinterland and are ideal for wilderness fishing.

Right: The old stamper battery in the Karangahake Gorge (Auckland/ Waikato region) crushed gold out of quartz rock. In the Ohinemuri River below there are fly fishing riches of both brown and rainbow trout.

Above: A pleasant way to break for lunch or relax after that early morning fishing trip in the Taupo region, outdoor dining on Cherry Island, Waikato River.

Below: Trolling for trout on Lake Taupo is one of the more relaxing – and productive – ways to go fishing. It is also the best way to explore remote shorelines.

Right: A perfect mountain and a perfect trout river. In Taranaki it can be hard to stay focused on fishing.

Below: You can't get much closer to a river than dam dropping on the Waingongoro River, near Hawera (Taranaki region), with Kaitiaki Adventures.

ROB TUCKER

ROB TUCKER

Above: Mt Ruapehu provides winter fun for skiers and snowboarders – and snowmelt water to feed an array of trout streams and rivers in the surrounding regions.

Left: Tongariro River, a world-renowned rainbow trout fishery in the Taupo region – and an excellent white water kayaking venue.

Taupo

Lake Taupo, the largest lake in New Zealand, is also the centre of the country's largest trout fishery. The lake acts like an inland sea, a vast fish-holding reservoir to feed the many rivers and streams that feed into it with fresh-run spawning trout, in the manner of the sea-run steelhead rainbow trout that were used to stock New Zealand waters.

FAMOUS FOR

- Trout fishing
- Wairakei Golf Course
- Huka Falls
- Thermal areas
- Mt Ruapehu
- Lake Taupo
- Tongariro River

On 24 February 1898, Forrestina Ross tipped a pannikinful of rainbow trout fry into the headwaters of the Tongariro River and began the cycle of fish migrating from river and stream to the lake and back to the rivers and streams to spawn. Trout did so well in the pristine environment that the size of catches soon became legendary. In one day in 1911 at the Waihaha mouth two merciless fish killers took 78 trout between them. A photograph shows the haul laid out in rows with no fish under 7.25 kg and the total weight of the catch 425.45 kg. American author Zane Grey, who fished Lake Taupo in 1925, was responsible for Taupo acquiring an international reputation as a premium wild fishery after his rapturous praise of fighting Taupo trout in his book *Tales of an Angler's El Dorado*.

The Taupo district is now a wild fishery, with no hatchery stocking, and fish weights have stabilised at around 1.58–2.2 kg. There are seasonal fluctuations depending on the size of resident stocks and the availability of food. Natural food supplies have been enhanced by the introduction of smelt. The lake holds thousands of fish at all depths, including those which can only be reached with downrigger equipment. Lake anglers account for 55 per cent of the total trout harvest.

There is extensive trolling and also a considerable amount of fly fishing from boats anchored at stream mouths. Over 100,000 trout larger than 45 cm

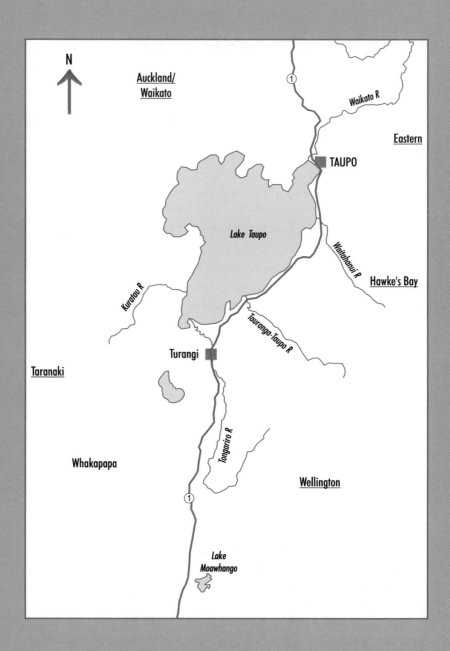

are caught each year. The Tongariro River is the main spawning river and Turangi, the town at the Tongariro Delta, proudly calls itself the Trout Fishing Capital of the World – and with some justification. Both Turangi and Taupo have a good range of motels and hotels, restaurants, tackle shops and fishing guides.

The Tongariro has been fished by dignitaries from around the world, and its pools, each steeped with history, carry such names as The Duchess Pool, The Major Jones Pool, The Admiral Pool, Judges and so on.

The Taupo Fishery has been developed in partnership with traditional Maori landowners, the Ngati Tuwharetoa, who hold title to the lakebed and much other land in the catchment. In 1926, in a special act of parliament, Ngati Tuwharetoa gave free public access to the lake and its tributaries in exchange for a fee equivalent to half the fishing licence fees received each year. Consequently, the Taupo fishery, which is managed by the Department of Conservation, must be fished with a special licence, and nearly $1 million a year from the more than 63,000 licences issued annually goes to the iwi [tribe].

INFORMATION

Department of Conservation
Taupo Fishery Area Office
Private Bag
Turanga Place
Turangi
07 386 8607
07 386 7086 (fax)
www.doc.govt.nz
Area manager: John Gibbs

Turangi Visitor Information Centre
Ngawaka Place
Turangi
07 386 8999
turangivc@laketauponzcom
www.ruapehunz.com

Taupo Visitor Information Centre
30 Tongariro Street
Taupo
07 376 0027

Destination Lake Taupo
66 Paora Hapi Street
Taupo
07 376 0400
www.laketauponz.com

Tongariro National Trout Society
Gordon Stevenson
8 Kapua Place
Taupo
07 378 8473
gordons@reap.org.nz

The volcanic explosion that blew the 618 sq km lake out to a depth of 185 m 2000 years ago was so violent that the crimson skies in the Southern Hemisphere were noted by Roman and Chinese historians. Volcanic activity still plays a part in the fishery today. The Tongariro River, the major river feeding the lake, is fed by the snow melt of the central North Island mountain trio of Mt Tongariro, Mt Ngauruhoe and Mt Ruapehu. Volcanic ash and pumice – a super-heated and aerated form of lava stone – tends to be the underlying ground in streams and around the lake shore, and it is not unusual for river anglers to see lumps of pumice float by.

WHERE AND WHAT

The Taupo Fishing District lies within the Tongariro/Taupo Conservancy of the Department of Conservation. The fishery boundary roughly equates to a line drawn around Lake Taupo and its catchment area so as to include those rivers and streams that feed into the lake.

Lake Taupo and the river mouths are open for fishing all year round. Many of the more than 40 rivers and streams that flow into the lake are open year-round as well. However, most of the upper reaches are closed to fishing between 31 June and 1 December when rainbow trout return to the rivers and streams to spawn. Some other lakes in the Taupo District, such as Otamangakau, are also closed between 31 June and 1 December.

Rainbows predominate but browns are found in most rivers and lakes in the district. The browns tend to make their spawning runs during summer and autumn. The daily catch is limited to three fish and 45 cm is the minimum length. Much of the fishing in the district is easily accessible by car and/or boat. Helicopter and raft fishing is readily available for more remote areas.

Taupo waters are mostly snowmelt-fed and even in summer the water can be cold – neoprene chest waders are advisable. River and stream banks tend to be infested with brambles and blackberries and waders made from lightweight material are easily damaged.

In summer and early autumn there is exciting fishing around the river mouths and shoreline shallows as trout chase shoals of smelt. Summer is also the best time for dry fly fishing.

Catch and release is actively encouraged in all waters except Lake Taupo and the main rivers, where there is good evidence from DoC monitoring that without 'culling' trout populations build faster than the feed available.

Casting around

LAKE TAUPO

With 160 km of shoreline, there are immense opportunities for fishing around the lake edge. Kuratau, Waihaha beach and White Cliffs are particularly productive because of the concentrations of smelt. The mouths of the many small streams that flow into the lake produce good results, especially at dusk or in the early morning. Other noted shoreline fishing spots are the boat harbour, near the entrance to the Waikato River, Two Mile Bay and Four Mile Bay.

Harling a smelt pattern fly around the shallow lake margins in spring and early summer when spawning trout are returning to the lake is effective. So is deep trolling with lead core lines. The fish are at about 12 m deep and with the 100 m of lead line and 100 m of backing needed to get there, it can be a bit like fishing a sack of potatoes. Other noted lake fishing spots are Stump Bay, at the southern end of the lake, Whareroa River mouth, Whangamata Bay and Acacia Bay.

The Waitahanui River

The Waitahanui is renowned among Taupo fishers for the large browns that hide along its overhung banks. It is springfed so it usually runs clear and the bed is mostly pumice and fine shingle – unlike the boulderstrewn bottoms found elsewhere in the fishery.

You can never pass the river mouth on SH1, 11 km south of Taupo, without seeing a 'picket fence' of fishers casting

TACKLE BOX

Sporting Life
The Mall
Turangi
07 386 8996
sport.life@xtra.co.nz
www.sportinglife-turangi.co.nz

The Fly and Gun
18 Heu Heu Street
Taupo
07 378 4449

Greenstone Fishing
47 Tongariro Street
Taupo
07 378 3714

Taupo Rod & Tackle
7 Tongariro Street
Taupo
07 378 5337

Creel Tackle House
189 Taupahi Road
Turangi
07 386 7929

into the flow as it runs into Lake Taupo. The 'picket fence' is famous among anglers but so too is the 8 km of fine fishing water upstream. The most convenient tracks to some pools often take a direct route through Maori land and it is both courteous and prudent to ensure that access is permitted. The public are entitled to free foot access through the Wharekawa Scenic Reserve which follows the true left bank of the river from the SH1 bridge up to Butlers Bend. The rest of the river has a 20 m-wide right of way on both banks for licensed anglers travelling on foot. Anglers' access was negotiated in the 1926 agreement with the Ngati Tuwharetoa, although in recent years some members of a hapu [sub-tribe] living at Waitahanui have claimed they were not party to the agreement and have challenged anglers. There is never any shortage of anglers on the Waitahanui – including many locals – so there is no difficulty in seeking advice on access. DoC advise that any anglers threatened over access to the Waitahanui should report the matter to the Taupo Police.

GUIDES AND CHARTERS

Peter Church
13 Rangiamohia Road
Turangi
07 386 8621

Greg Catley
PO Box 1585
Taupo
07 377 0035
u2fishtaupo@xtra.co.nz
www.nzflyfish.co.nz

Tony Hayes
PO Box 278
Turangi
07 3867946
trout@reap.org.nz
www.tongarirolodge.co.nz

Simon Dickie
PO Box 682
Taupo
07 378 9680
simondickie@reap.org.nz

Chris Jolly
PO Box 1020
Taupo
07 378 0623

Tim McCarthy
PO Box 89
Turangi
07 386 8207

Graham Pyatt
Grace Road
Turangi
07 386 6032
grahampyatt@xtra.co.nz
www.fishnhunt.co.nz/trout/

Carol Harwood
PO Box 290
Turangi
07 386 7929
www.fishingtaupo.co.nz

Kerry Simpson
155 Tuapahi Road
Turangi
07 386 7341

Te Moana Charters
215 Tamamutu Street
Taupo
07 378 4839

Graham Dean
c/o The Store
Te Rangiita
Turangi
07 386 0726

Sadly, there are other problems with this famous trout river too. The river is mainly fished with nymph and wet fly, and because of its popularity it has the potential for conflict between anglers, particularly in the lower reaches. The Waitahanui has a reputation for bringing out the best in fishing and the worst in anglers. Some long-time Waitahanui anglers treat the river as their personal fiefdom and become possessive about certain pools.

Best runs are usually from July to September.

THE HINEMAIAIA RIVER

The Hinemaiaia winds from the high plateau through a steep-sided valley to reach Lake Taupo at Hatepe. It is considered a big-fish river and is popular with both wet fly and nymph. The mouth is usually productive throughout the year, particularly after dark. The river is closed to angling above SH1 from 1 June until 30 November.

THE TAURANGA-TAUPO RIVER

The Tauranga-Taupo is possibly second only to the nearby Tongariro River as the most productive in the Taupo fishery. It is a large river with both excellent mouth fishing and many kilometres of pools and reaches upstream. In the lower reaches it is prone to flooding and changing its course, but it often keeps fishing well when other waters have gone cold. The lower reaches are fairly open and provide relatively easy casting for novice anglers. Further upstream is rugged, wilderness-style fishing. The mouth is usually too deep to wade but fishes well from a dinghy, particularly after dark.

THE WAIMARINO STREAM

This is a delightful stream that usually demands a delicate presentation. The mouth fishes well at night.

STUMP BAY

This is the weedy, insect-rich area of Lake Taupo from the Waimarino mouth to the Tongariro Delta. It is a top feeding ground but can be difficult to fish.

THE TONGARIRO RIVER

The Tongariro has been called the greatest trout stream in the world. It vies with the Mataura in Southland as being the most famous of all New Zealand's trout-fishing waters. The Mataura is known for its browns; and the Tongariro for the fighting rainbows that moved Zane Grey to gushy superlatives. It is a big rambunctious river fed by snowmelt from the three peaks of Tongariro National Park, although the flow is now artificially tempered by the Tongariro Power Scheme.

The Tongariro's many pools are legendary, as are some of the spawning streams that run into it. From May onwards fresh runs of spawning rainbows will stream up the Tongariro from Lake Taupo following periods of rain. But there are also resident fish in the river. Downstream wet fly and upstream nymph are the most popular methods for winter fishing but during summer months there is good dry fly fishing in the lower reaches. The fishing is predominantly rainbows but some big browns are taken on the dry fly in summer, particularly during the evening rise. Some pools – notably The Hydro – are noted for holding browns.

The many pools on the Tongariro – including over 40 named pools – are generally divided into upper, middle and lower, with Turangi township being roughly around the middle pools. The river is well signposted and maps of

CATCH A MEAL

Cajun-Kiwi Licensed Restaurant
Roberts Street
Taupo
07 378 5276
creole cooking from a genuine New Orleans chef

The Bach
Pataka Road
Lake Terrace
Taupo
07 378 7856
views of the sunset to go with oven-fired gourmet pizza

Santorinis
133 Tongariro Street
Taupo
07 377 2205
Greek and Mediterranean cuisine

Villino Restaurant
Horomatangi Street
Taupo
07 377 4478
www.villino.co.nz
for a romantic evening

CATCH A MEAL

Parklands Motor Lodge
cnr State Highway 1 and Arahori
Turangi
07 386 7515
info@prklands.co.nz
www.prklands.co.nz
licensed restaurant and bar

The Grand Chateau
Whakapapa Village
Mt Ruapehu
0800 242 832
reservations@chateau.co.nz
www.chateau.co.nz
elegance and style

Tokaanu Resort Hotel
Tokaanu
07 386 8873
tokaanu.hotel@xtra.co.nz
www.tokaanuhotel.co.nz
à la carte restaurant

Tongariro Lodge
Grace Road
Turangi
07 386 8555
www.tongarirolodge.co.nz
fish and game

the pools are generally available at tackle shops. Periodic flooding will change the nature of some pools but generally they remain the same. There is a legal right of way 20 m from the river edge, a good walking track on both sides of the river and two footbridges as well as the SH1 road bridge. The last of the upper pools is the Whitikau, which tends to hold many fish waiting for the right time to run into the Whitikau Stream to spawn. In the season you can fish the waters beyond the Whitikau with raft-fishing guides.

Each of the Tongariro pools has its own peculiarities, requiring differing techniques. Most pools are deep and there is a strong water flow, so long leaders and a weighted nymph are needed to get to the bottom quickly. Wet fly fishermen use an ultra-fast sinking shooting head line. Some pools are more popular than others, leading to congestion and – sadly – the occasional fracas. And some anglers consistently fish only their 'favourite pool'. But there are fish moving in the Tongariro most of the time, as well as resident fish, and it is possible to ignore the crowds and still get good catches if you happen to be exploring a tempting reach at just the right time. In the summer there is good dry fly fishing in the lower reaches of the river where willows hang over the banks.

THE TONGARIRO DELTA

The river delta has its own picket fence – a line-up of anchored boats where anglers fish a small drop-off with a slowly mended smelt imitation fly. A very productive spot that usually never fails to produce fish.

HANG YOUR HOOK

Paeroa Lakeside Homestay
21 Te Kopua Street
Acacia Bay
Taupo
07 378 8449
bibby@reap.org.nz
www.taupohomestay.com
lakefront luxury with private beach, lake views and resident boat and guide

Five Mile Bay Homestay
60 Mahuta Road
Five Mile Bay
RD2 Taupo
07 378 0663
hughes.jbk@xtra.co.nz
on the lakeshore, two minutes from the Waitahanui Stream

Huka Lodge
Huka Falls Road
Taupo
07 378 5791
reservations@hukalodge.co.nz
luxury on the banks of the Waikato River

Lanecove Hotel
213 Lake Terrace
Taupo
07 378 7599
info@lanecove.co.nz
www.lanecove.co.nz
boutique cental hotel on the lakefront

Waitahanui Lodge
State Highway 1
Waitahanui
07 378 7183
cosy lakeside cottages

The Art of Roosting
Parerohi Grove
Pukawa Bay
Taupo
07 386 6112
peace and quiet with panoramic views

Creel Lodge Motels
183–187 Taupahi Road
Turangi
07 386 8081
backs onto the Tongariro River

Sportsmans Lodge
15 Taupehi Road
Turangi
07 386 8150
sportsmanslodge@xtra.co.nz
inexpensive comfort on the banks of the Tongariro River

Windsor Lodge
State Highway 1
Waitahanui
Taupo
07 378 6271
windsor.lodge@xtra.co.nz
www.windsorlodge.co.nz
long-standing haven for Taupo anglers

Anglers Paradise Resort
cnr State Highway 41 and Ohuanga Road
Turangi
07 386 8980
anglers@reap.org.nz
every facility – including licensed restaurant

River Birches
21 Koura Street
Turangi
07 386 5348
gillo@voyager.co.nz
cosy two-bedroomed, serviced cottage

Tongariro Lodge
Grace Road
PO Box 278
Turangi
07 386 7946
trout@reap.org.nz
US Presidents have stayed in this lodge on the banks of the Tongariro River

TOKAANU TAILRACE

The tailrace of the Tokaanu Electric Power Station can fish well when the turbines are running. At worst, it is an excellent place to practise fly casting.

TOKAANU WHARF

This is a relic of the days when steamships plied the lake, although the wharf has been recently renovated. It is often a good spot for smelt flies on a floating line – and casting is never a problem.

LAKE OTAMANGAKAU

A shallow, reed-infested lake south of Lake Taupo created in 1971 by the Tongariro Power Project that is famed for holding trophy-sized fish. The lake, once a swamp area until some water diverted from the Whakapapa and Wanganui Rivers turned it into a flooded highland moor, has yielded trout of more than 8 kg. The lake has an abundance of insects to fatten cruising trout and a huge cicada hatch. The lake is mainly fished wading the shallows using a floating line and lures to simulate wind-fallen insects. It has also proved ideal for fishing using a float tube. And if the fishing ever fails, the scenery is majestic.

LAKE ROTOAIRA

A gem of a lake south of Turangi just over the Pihanga Saddle between SH47 and SH46. You need an additional licence for this Maori-owned lake, which you can purchase at tackle shops in Turangi, but it is usually worth the cost. Shore access is limited so most fishing is by trolling or casting from a boat. However, good catches are taken regularly casting from the shore near the intake to the Tokaanu tailrace, particularly during cicada hatches. The mouths of the hydro diversion canals which feed into the lake from the Tongariro River and Lake Otamangakau usually provide the best fishing. The small island in the lake, Motuopuhi, is famous as being the spot where the Maori warlord, Te Rauparaha, composed the haka 'Ka mate' used by the New Zealand All Blacks rugby team.

WHEN THE FISH DON'T BITE

Kiwi Outback Tours
State Highway 46
Turangi
0800 628 642
*horse treks and 4x4 bike treks on Mt
Tongariro*

Tongariro River Rafting
Turangi
0800 101 024
www.whitewaterraft.co.nz
*daily rafting on the Tongariro – raft fishing
in season*

Rock'n'river Rafting
203 Puanga Street
Tokaanu
0800 865 2266
rock.n.river@xtra.co.nz
www.RaftingNewZealand.com
*adventure rafting followed by hot pools at
the Tokaanu base*

Huka Jet
Wairakei Park
Taupo
0800 485 2538
www.hukajet.co.nz
*spin into the spray from the foaming Huka
Falls*

Army Museum
State Highway 1
Waiouru
0800 369 999
Elizabeth.Cottrell@nzdf.mil.nz
*the story of the New Zealand army from
Gate Pa to Vietnam*

Prawn Park
Wairakei Park
Taupo
07 374 8474
prawn@reap.org.nz
*fresh prawns from the world's only
geothermally-heated prawn farm*

Orakei-Korako Hidden Valley
494 Orakei-Korako Road
Taupo
07 378 3131
ok@reap.org.nz
www.orakeikorako.co.nz
*unspoilt geothermal wonderland with huge
silica terraces*

Whakapapa Ski Area
Bruce Road
Whakapapa
Mt Ruapehu
07 892 3738
www.MtRuapehu.com
*winter skiing and snowboarding; summer
sightseeing.*

Taupo Bungy
Spa Road
Taupo
0800 888 408
www.taupobungy.com
jump like a fighting river trout

National Trout Centre
State Highway 1
Turangi
*watch trout feeding from an underwater
viewing chamber*

Taranaki

Few regions anywhere are blessed with such a superbly distinctive visual icon as is Taranaki. If you ask any child to paint a picture of a mountain then you can be almost certain the drawing will bear a striking resemblance to Mt Taranaki. The near-perfect andesite volcano rising alone – 2518 m out of a plain of greenest farmland – is a dreamer's mountain.

Maori explain its isolation with a tale of a clash by rival suitors for the love of Mt Pihanga that stands behind Turangi. Taranaki lost and was kicked out of the Central North Island volcanic region by the victor, Tongariro, carving out the Whanganui River as it fled west. But for being blocked by the Pouakai Ranges, Taranaki would have vanished into the sea in its despair. Instead it has stood magnificently (and quietly) for the past 225 years, overlooking bloody intertribal clashes among Maori and rapacious land grabbing by Pakeha. The mountain heights were tapu to Maori and have long been revered by Pakeha. In 1881 all land within 9.6 km of the summit became protected and more than 100 years ago the cone and its ring of alpine scrubland and thick forest became Egmont National Park – the second-oldest national park in New Zealand.

Named Mt Egmont by Captain James Cook – and still fiercely called that by some diehard provincials – Mt Taranaki is surrounded by lush pasture that feeds a vibrant dairy industry which supplies the biggest dairy factory in the

FAMOUS FOR

- Mt Taranaki
- Oil and gas wells
- Rhododendrons
- Surf beaches
- Dairy cows
- Flower gardens
- Pukekura Park
- Parihaka
- Bridge to Nowhere
- Whanganui River

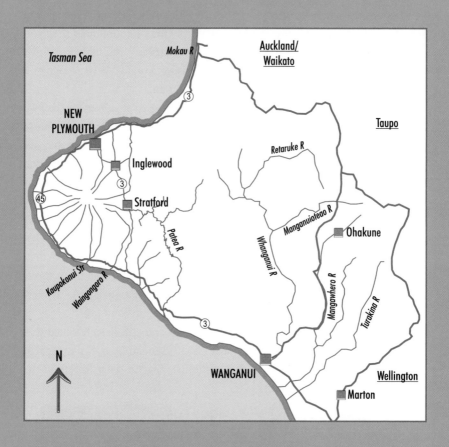

Tasman Sea

Mokau R

Auckland/
Waikato

③

NEW
PLYMOUTH

Taupo

Inglewood

③

Retaruke R

Stratford

Patea R

Manganuioteao R

Ohakune

Whanganui R

Kaupokonui Str

Mangawhero R

Turakina R

Waingongoro R

③

N

WANGANUI

Wellington

Marton

④⑤

world. The region flows with milk – and oil from both onshore and offshore wells. It also flows with some excellent trout streams and rivers.

The streams in the ringplain around Mt Taranaki are excellent for stalking large brown trout. There are also several lakes holding rainbows. To the west are rivers and streams that flow out of the high country of the Whanganui National Park. The region also includes the area to the south of Mt Ruapehu which mainly feeds into the Whanganui River and provides excellent wilderness fishing.

An attractive feature of the trout fishing in the region is that the waters are uncrowded. Compared with other regions, few anglers seem to try their luck in Taranaki. It is significant that in the preparation of this book, we were unable to locate any trout-fishing guides specialising in the region. Another characteristic of the region is its fishing diversity – anglers can sight-fish for brown trout in small streams on Mt Taranaki, target the evening rise on large boulder-strewn rivers in the Ruapehu area, or go boat fishing on lakes near

INFORMATION

Fish and Game New Zealand Taranaki Region
1H Taupo Quay
PO Box 4152
Wanganui
06 345 4908

290A Devon Street East
PO Box 662
New Plymouth
06 757 9676
fg-wan@clear.net.nz
www.fishandgame.org.nz
Manager: Peter Hill
Field Officers: Allen Stancliff and Miranda Robinson

Wanganui Visitor Information Centre
101 Guyton Street
Wanganui
06 349 0508
www.wanganuinz.com

DoC Whanganui
cnr Ingestra and Guyton Streets
Wanganui
06 345 2402
www.doc.govt.nz

New Plymouth Visitor Information Centre
cnr Leach and Liardet Streets
New Plymouth
06 759 6080
info@newplymouth.govt.nz
www.newplymouthnz.com

Destination Taranaki
PO Box 290
New Plymouth
06 757 9909
taranakinz@xtra.co.nz
www.taranakinz.org

Wanganui. As well, many of Taranaki's trout waters originate in National Parks and the water quality is excellent.

And whether for a weekend or a week, there is no shortage of things to do in the region between casting a fly or spinner. The radial pattern of more than 30 trout streams around Mt Taranaki means that anglers and their families have opportunities for a wide range of activities without too much travelling. The sea – and some of the best surf beaches in New Zealand – is close at hand, as are the Whanganui and Tongariro National Parks. Combining a fishing trip in Taranaki with other outdoor adventures such as surfing, mountain climbing and tramping is practical and effortless.

WHERE AND WHAT

Fish and Game New Zealand's Taranaki territory encompasses the entire Taranaki region, and a bit more besides. It stretches from the Mokau River in the north, west to the mountains of the Tongariro National Park and south-west to include the western catchments of the Whanganui River. There is a good diversity of trout fishing in the region yet, compared with other regions in New Zealand, there are very few anglers.

In the east of the district the many streams in the ringplain around Mt Taranaki offer good sight-fishing opportunities for large brown trout, particularly in the upper reaches of streams. Most small and medium-sized waters hold around 10 good fish per kilometre, which roughly works out at one to two trout per pool. Taranaki browns often reach 2 kg or more. There are four catch-and-release sections around the mountain.

Wanganui has several lakes that provide fishing for perch and rainbow trout within a few minutes of the city. Rainbow trout fishing is also available at Lakes Mangamahoe and Ratapiko, and the Waingongoro River between Eltham and the sea supports a good population of rainbow. While Taranaki has an extensive network of sealed roads, there are few marginal strips or esplanade reserves along streams in rural areas and access for fishing usually requires getting landowner permission to cross farmland. Fortunately, anglers and landowners maintain a good relationship in Taranaki and access is seldom denied. Most streams are fishable within 24–36 hours of rain and, owing to the rain shadow effect, it is not often that all streams are unfishable at any one time.

In the south-west of the region, the Ruapehu district rivers support some of the most productive fisheries in the region, with none more so than the Manganuioteao – a nationally important brown and rainbow trout fishery that offers superb wilderness fishing and spectacular scenery.

Information pamphlets on Taranaki Region trout fisheries are available at most sports shops and information centres within the region, and from Taranaki Fish and Game offices in Wanganui and New Plymouth.

The Taranaki Region's regulations

follow the general North Island sports fishing regulations. Open for fishing all year round are Lake Rotomanu, Lake Mangamahoe (excluding the Waiwhakaiho inlet); Lake Ngangana, Opunake Lake, Virginia Lake, Lake Namunamu; the Waiwhakaiho River downstream from the end of Rimu Street extension; Huatoki Stream downstream from Brois Street bridge; Waitara River downstream from the Manganui River confluence; Whanganui River (excluding tributaries); Mangawhero River (excluding tributaries) downstream from the 'golf course' bridge at SH49; Tokiahuru Stream downstream from the bridge at SH49; Waitaiki Stream downstream from the bridge at SH49.

Fishing between 30 June and 1 October is prohibited in the Manganuioteao River and its tributaries; Retaruke River and its tributaries; Tokiahuru Stream upstream from the bridge at SH49; Waitaiki Stream upstream from the bridge at SH49; Mangawhero River and its tributaries upstream from the 'golf course' bridge at SH49; Raetihi Hydro Dam.

No fishing during May is allowed in Lake Rotorangi from the dam face to the Mangamingi ramp; Lake Ratapiko, except the inlet race; Stony (Hangatahua) River, Warea River, Kapoaiaia Stream, Waiaua River, Mangahume Stream, Otakeho Stream, Kaupokonui Stream, Waingongoro River, all downstream from the SH45 bridges; Patea River downstream from Patea Dam; Lahar Lake.

Lake Wiritoa and Lake Pauri are closed for fishing from 20 April to 10 July. All other waters in the region are closed from 30 April until 1 October. Lake Mangamahoe, including the Waiwhakaiho inlet is restricted to fly fishing only. The Mangaoraka Stream from the bridge at Te Arei Road West upstream to the bridge at Corbett Road; Kai Auahi Stream upstream of the bridge at Alfred Road; Kapuni Stream upstream from the bridge at Skeet Road, are for catch-and-release fishing only.

On the Stony (Hangatahua) River from its source to the sea, brown trout must be released but a limit of two rainbows is allowed. A daily bag limit of two trout applies to Virginia Lake; Lake Ngangana; Lake Wiritoa; Lake Namunamu; Raetihi Hydro Dam; Lahar Lake; Manganuioteao River and its tributaries; all waters originating on the slopes of Mt Taranaki, including Lakes Mangamahoe, Rotomanu, Opunake, Ratapiko and Rotorangi, and the Waingongoro River downstream from Eltham Road. Elsewhere in the region the daily limit is four trout. There is no minimum length for trout caught in Taranaki.

Casting around

MT TARANAKI RINGPLAIN

Generally there are few 'Queen's Chain' reserves adjoining to ringplain waterways and anglers must obtain permission to cross private farmland. Landowners seldom deny access when asked.

Waiwhakaiho River

New Plymouth's closest river is best fished in its upper reaches, or in the lower river below the outlet of Mangorei power station. The Waiwhakaiho is subject to rapid rises in river level with heavy rainfall on the mountain. Access to the upper river is through farmland off Alfred or Egmont Roads, with bridge crossings at upper Lepper Road and SH3 (Egmont Village). Access to the lower river is from Devon Road (SH3) and Rimu Street, Merrilands Domain and William Street, which are all off Mangorei Road. At Rimu Street, head right at the fork in the road and walk along the gravel track at the end of the road. The pool at the end of the gravel track marks the upstream limit for all-year fishing. Large brown trout in the upper reaches are best targeted with a dry fly during the evening rise.

Kai Auahi Stream

This Waiwhakaiho River tributary provides challenging nymph and dry fly fishing for large browns up to 2.6 kg. The Kai Auahi above Alfred Road bridge is catch and release only. Access is best through farmland on the true left-hand

TACKLE BOX

Hawera Sportsworld
21 Union Street
Hawera
06 278 5530

Taranaki Hunting & Fishing
178 Gill Street
New Plymouth
06 757 2255

Stirling Sports
Shop 14
Centre City
New Plymouth
06 758 0964

Kiwi Outdoors Centre
18 Ariki Street
New Plymouth
06 758 4152

Ohakune Sports
957 Raetihi Road
Ohakune
06 385 8411

side of Alfred Road and from the Alfred Road bridge. The upper Kai Auahi is reached through farmland off Hill Road, which is off Albert Road.

Lake Rotomanu

This fishery near the Waiwhakaiho River mouth in New Plymouth, is stocked with takeable rainbow trout in late September each year. Anglers have easy access to the entire lake margin. Proceed east along Devon Street East, through the lights at Fitzroy and into Clemow Road, which leads to the lake.

Lake Mangamahoe

Between New Plymouth and Inglewood on SH3, Lake Mangamahoe is the region's most popular lake fishery. Brown trout up to 2.6 kg and rainbows up to 2.25 kg are present. Turn off SH3 onto a gravel road that runs along the western shoreline. Trout often cruise the lake margin in shallow water and a number of bays provide good fishing. Lake Mangamahoe is designated fly fishing only with fly rod and fly line.

Stony River

The Stony, near Okato in coastal Taranaki, has the best water quality of any ringplain fishery but suffered from major erosion in its headwaters in 1998. The habitat has stabilised and the river now holds reasonable numbers of hatchery rainbow trout and a few wild browns. The entire river has been made catch-and-release for brown trout to help the population recover. The daily bag limit for rainbow trout has been set at two fish. The lower river is reached from the Surf Highway bridge, through farmland off lower Kaihihi Road, or through farmland at the end of Brophy Road. The middle reaches are accessed via the Stony River walkway off upper Kaihihi Road and from the Mangatete Road bridge. The upper river is reached from Wiremu Road bridge (off Saunders Road) or from the top of Saunders or Puniho Roads. *Deleatidium* mayflies are the most common invertebrate and nymph, or dry fly fishing during the evening rise is recommended.

Maketawa Stream

Located 4 km south of Inglewood on SH3, the Maketawa has good water quality and holds brown trout up to 2.5 kg. The stream is reached from the

SH3 and Junction Road bridges (difficult) and through farmland off upper and lower Norfolk Road. Nymphing with small hare and copper, halfback and caddis patterns is most popular.

Lake Ratapiko

This shallow 21 ha hydro reservoir is 9 km down Tariki Road, which turns off SH3 midway between Inglewood and Stratford. The lake holds good populations of hatchery rainbows and wild brown trout that reach up to 3 kg. Small spinners will take fish. Nymph and wet fly fishing are also effective. The water-ski and power boat club areas off Tariki Road provide good access to the lake margin. Permission to fish from other areas should be obtained from the appropriate landowner.

Patea River

Running through the heart of Stratford, the Patea is one of the ringplain's most productive brown trout fisheries. Good fishing is available within Stratford township, though the largest fish are present below Skinner Road. Large browns and a few rainbows are present in the river below Patea Dam. There is plenty of fishable water between McColl's bridge and the dam face. The upper river is best fished from tracks within King Edward Park and along the walkway between Juliet Street and Swansea Road.

HANG YOUR HOOK

Powderhorn Chateau
bottom of Mountain Road
Ohakune
06 385 8888
powderhorn@xtra.co.nz
reminiscent of European alpine lodges with fine dining

Cairnbrae House Homestay
140 Mangawhero River Road
Ohakune
06 385 3002
peterm@cairnbrae house.co.nz
www.cairnbraehouse.co.nz
overlooks Cairnbrae deer park and Mt Ruapehu

Whare Ora
14 Kaha Street
Ohakune
06 385 9385
whareora@xtra.co.nz
located at the base of Mt Ruapehu with views to Mt Taranaki

Oak Valley Manor
248 Junction Road
RD1 New Plymouth
06 758 1501
inspiring views of Mt Taranaki

Henwood House
314 Henwood Road
New Plymouth
06 755 1212
henwood.house@xtra.co.nz
tastefully restored 19th-century mansion, and breakfast to die for

Patuha Farm Lodge
575 Upper Pitone Road
Okato
06 752 4469
patuha.farm.lodge@clear.net.nz
modern lodge on a family farm bordering Egmont National Park

HANG YOUR HOOK

Mountain House
Pembroke Road
Stratford
06 765 6100
mountainhouse@xtra.co.nz
*in the heart of Egmont National
Park at the foot of Mt Taranaki*

The Rutland Arms Inn
48–52 Ridgeway Street
Wanganui
06 347 7677
enquiries@rutland_arms.co.nz
historic hotel dating from 1849

The Gables
179 Fitzherbert Ave
Palmerston North
06 358 3209
*seclusion only 800 m from the
central business district*

Waitotara Country House
Waitotara
RD18 Wanganui
06 346 5749
www.remoteadventures.co.nz
*comfortable accommodation in
the wilderness*

Operiki
River Road 3302
RD6 Wanganui
06 342 8159
*comfy farmstay overlooking the
Whanganui River*

Ahu Ahu Beach Villas
Ahu Ahu Road
Oakura
06 752 7370
holiday@ahu.co.nz
www.ahu.co.nz
*villas that are works of art on a
stunning cliff-top site*

The middle reaches are accessed from Skinner Road bridge and through farmland off Bird, Hungers and Waihapa Roads. The lower Patea is reached via Ball Road, which runs off SH3 just north of Kakaramea. All methods work well.

Lake Rotorangi

This scenic 46 km-long hydro lake east of Eltham has few trout in its middle and lower reaches but the upper reaches from Glen Nui up to the first river rapid can produce good-conditioned browns and rainbows up to 2.25 kg. Access to the upper reaches is via Anderson and Rawhitiroa Roads at Eltham. There is a good boat-ramp at Glen Nui. The middle reaches are accessed via Tawhiti, Ararata and Tangahoe Valley Roads. The lower reaches via Ball Road off SH3. Deep trolling is the preferred fishing method.

Waingongoro River

Located on the south-eastern slopes of Mt Taranaki, the Waingongoro River is the most popular ringplain fishery. In its upper reaches, it is a clear mountain stream supporting up to 20 takeable browns per km. Below Eltham, the Waingongoro is tannin-stained, but supports the ringplain's most productive rainbow trout fishery and is great for beginners. The upper river is accessed from the Cardiff walkway upstream of Opunake Road, from Finnerty and

Cornwall Roads off SH3 and from road ends off Collingwood Street within Eltham township. Access to the middle and lower reaches is via a handful of road ends and bridge crossings off SH3, including Rogers Road off Dalziell Road, Skeet, Mawhitiwhiti and Normanby Roads and SH45. Nymph and dry fly fishing is best in the upper reaches. All methods work well in the middle and lower reaches, including spin fishing. Caddis imitations for the evening rise are recommended.

Kapuni Stream

This stream provides high-quality sight-fishing opportunities for large brown trout, particularly in the upper reaches. The Kapuni above Skeet Road bridge

CATCH A MEAL

Marinovich's Seafood Restaurant and Café
19 Broughton Street
New Plymouth
06 758 4749
seafood

Metropol Café Restaurant Bar and Grill
cnr King and Egmont Streets
New Plymouth
06 758 9788
New Zealand cuisine

Mountain House Restaurant
Pembroke Road
Egmont National Park
06 765 6100
mountainhouse@xtra.co.nz
www.mountainhouse.co.nz
recipes from the Swiss Alps

Portofino
14 Gill Street
New Plymouth
06 757 8686
Italian

Salvation
Devon Street
New Plymouth
06 759 1626
www.salvation.co.nz
Thai and Japanese

Zanziba Café and Bar
440 Devon Street East
New Plymouth
06 757 8147
www.zanziba.co.nz
pizzas and more

Alpine à la carte
25 Somme Parade
Wanganui
06 348 7450
Reservations@LegendsCafe.co.nz
judged best in Wanganui

Utopia Café
47 Clyde Street
Ohakune
06 385 9120
scarface@ihug.co.nz
killer wine selection

is catch-and-release only. The upper river is reached from Palmer and Eltham Road bridges, or through farmland off Palmer Road; Kokiri and Normanby Road bridges provide access to the lower reaches. Fly fishing with small hare and copper or halfback nymphs, brown and green beetle imitations, Coch-y-Bondhu or caddis dry flies are effective.

Kaupokonui Stream

The Kaupokonui, 5 km west of Manaia, and its largest tributary – the Mangawhero Stream – both contain good-sized brown trout, with the odd rainbow. The Kaupokonui is fished from bridge crossings at Eltham, Skeet and Upper Glenn Roads and the Surf Highway, or through farmland off Manaia Road. The Mangawhero is best fished above and below the Skeet Road bridge, or by crossing the Kaupokonui a short distance upstream of the Surf Highway, or through farmland off Upper Glenn or Rama Roads. Nymph, dry fly, or bait fishing with creeper and worm are recommended.

WANGANUI FISHERIES

Virginia Lake

North of Wanganui on SH3, this scenic lake is stocked with takeable rainbow trout in late September each year. Fishing is reserved for child, junior and young adult licence holders only.

Lake Namunamu

This pristine 13 ha lake is on private property 14 km west of Hunterville on Turakina Valley Road. The lake is stocked each year and contains good-conditioned rainbows up to 2 kg. Park by the Lake Namunamu signpost. It is then a 20-minute uphill walk along a good farm track. It is best to harl a sinking line and lure from one of the dinghies left at the lake.

Lower Mangawhero River

The lower Mangawhero, which runs beside SH4 for much of its length, has good fishing for brown trout averaging 1.5 kg. The river is best fished during dry spells, when it is relatively clear.

Whanganui River Estuary

Each season, a number of large sea or estuarine-run brown trout have been caught within the Wanganui City limits. Even the occasional salmon has been caught near the river mouth. The eastern bank can be accessed from SH4 and further upstream from the Wanganui River Road. The western bank is accessed from a number of roads within Wanganui City. Spinning is preferred, although the use of large wet flies at dusk will also be effective.

RUAPEHU FISHERIES

Manganuioteao River

Granted a National Water Conservation Order in 1989, the Manganuioteao River near Raetihi supports a nationally significant fishery for brown and rainbow trout, averaging 1.5 kg. The level of angling use is low by national standards and there are always good fishing areas available. Ohura Road, about 4 km north of Raetihi on SH4, leads to the river. Makakahi, Ruatiti and Pukekaha Roads branch off Ohura Road to the lower, middle and upper reaches respectively. River access and a free camping area are available at Ruatiti Domain; bridge crossings also provide access. A large sign at Ruatiti Domain shows the various property boundaries and anglers must get permission from the landowners. All fishing methods are popular. Daytime nymphing with weighted halfback, hare and copper and caddis imitations are recommended. Dry fly fishing with Coch-y-Bondhu, Brown Beetle, Black Gnat and Twilight Beauty patterns are favoured for the evening rise.

Upper Mangawhero River

The Mangawhero contains a good population of brown trout averaging 1.5 kg. The main fishing area is a 10 km reach between Ohakune and a gorge, which the river enters as it leaves the central plateau. Access is from within Ohakune township and from Old Mangarewa Road, SH49 and Pakihi Road. Nymph, dry and wet fly fishing are popular and the usual patterns work well. Fish rise mostly at dusk, although daytime activity occurs in December when brown and green beetles are abundant. The Mangawhero below the SH49 'golf course' bridge is open to all-year angling.

Taonui Stream

This small springfed stream joins the Mangawhero between Ohakune and
Raetihi. The Taonui holds brown trout averaging 2 kg throughout its length,
but it is fished mostly in the 4 km below the railway line. Access is from
SH49 and from Old Mangarewa Road near the Mangawhero confluence. All
methods are effective.

Retaruke River

This tannin-stained Whanganui River tributary west of Raurimu contains a
mixed population of brown and rainbow trout that average 1–2 kg, with the
occasional large fish. The upper Retaruke River provides at least 8 km of
good fly fishing water, which is best fished during the summer low-flow
period. The remaining 20 km of river down to the Whanganui junction is
more suited to spinning. Access is via the sealed Whakahora–Kaitieke Road,
which turns off SH4 just south of Owhango, or by an unsealed road off SH4
just south of Raurimu. At the Retaruke–Kaitieke confluence, turn left up
upper Retaruke Road for access to the upper river. Anglers can access the
riverbed via the scenic reserve or by obtaining permission from the
appropriate landowner. All methods will take fish, although fishing with
weighted nymphs is most popular.

Tokiahuru and Waitaiki Streams

The upper reaches of these fast-flowing Whangaehu tributaries contain a
dense population of small rainbow trout. Large trout are most abundant in
the 4 km of water between the Tokiahuru–Waitaiki confluence and the
Whangaehu River. These streams can often be fished when other waters are
discoloured by heavy rain, with best fishing from December to March. Both
streams are open all year below the SH49 bridges. Access to the Waitaiki is
from Karioi Station Road and Whangaehu Valley Road. The upper Tokiahuru
can be reached from the old forestry headquarters on SH49 between
Ohakune and Waiouru and the lower river from Whangaehu Valley–
Oruakukuru Road. Heavily weighted nymphs (hare and copper, halfback,
pheasant tail and caddis imitations) or a Tongariro-style two-nymph rig are
recommended.

WHEN THE FISH DON'T BITE

Mountain Guides, Mt Egmont
PO Box 783
New Plymouth
06 758 8261; 025 474 510
mguide@voyager.co.nz
www.mountainguides.co.nz
guided mountaineering, ski touring and hiking

Canoe Safaris
PO Box 180
Ohakune
06 385 9237
canoe@voyager.co.nz
www.canoesafaris.co.nz
canoe and kayak trips on the Whanganui River

Rangitikei River Adventures
State Highway 1
Mangaweka
06 382 5747
riveradventures@internet.co.nz
rafting the deep gorges of the Rangitikei River

Govett-Brewster Art Gallery
Queen Street
New Plymouth
06 758 5149
mail@govettbrewster.org.nz
www.govettbrewster.org.nz
Len Lye's kinetic sculptures

Happy Chaddy's Charters
Ocean View Parade
New Plymouth
06 758 9133
cruise to the Sugar Loaf Islands seal colony in the Bridlington lifeboat

Fun Ho Toy Museum
Rata Street
Inglewood
06 756 7030
www.funho.com
real kiwiana toys on display

Puketi Rhododendron Trust
Carrington Road
New Plymouth
06 752 4141
puketi@puketi.org.nz

Kaitiaki Adventures
Hawera
06 278 4452
darrenparata@bitworks.co.nz
www.kaitiaki.co.nz
sledge over a hydro dam

Tawhiti Museum
401 Ohangi Road
Hawera
06 278 6837
full-size mock-ups of scenes from yesterday

Whanganui River Boat Centre
1A Taupo Quay
Wanganui
06 347 1863
www.wanganui.co.nz/riverboats
cruise the Whanganui River on the PS Waimarie, the last paddle-steamer

Bridge to Nowhere Jetboat Tours
Pipiriki
RD6 Whanganui National Park
06 385 4128
Bridgetonowhere@paradise.net.nz
half-day wilderness river adventure

Wellington

Capital city – capital trout fishing? Well, not quite. There are trout to be had but the Wellington Fish and Game region is certainly not one of the renowned New Zealand trout fisheries. And yet it probably deserves to be, for the region is mostly a place for trout-fishing purists. To catch trout in the Wellington district you usually have to put in some effort, not sit on the back of a boat trolling a bit of plastic or metal around a lake.

The region's rivers rise in a spine of high country that bisects the district north to south and with not too much land to flow through before they reach the sea. Thus, much of the best fishing is in forest park wilderness, and while access is generally not a problem it does mean that anglers usually have to walk to get to their quarry. Of course, the reward for that is to be casting for trout in an uncrowded fishery among magnificent native bush and rugged mountain scenery.

Wellington enjoys another distinction that sets it apart from other North Island regions. It is almost exclusively a brown trout fishery. Browns were first introduced in 1874, and while rainbows were introduced around 1898 they have only become established in the Rangitikei River.

The Wellington region contains three of the country's top fishing waters. The Mangatainoka and Ruamahanga Rivers, which rise in the Tararua Ranges, and the Hutt River, which rises in the southern Tararuas and empties into Wellington Harbour, hold good stocks of brown trout that challenge and

FAMOUS FOR

- Rimutaka Incline
- Mount Bruce National Wildlife Centre
- The Beehive
- Strong winds

- The Capital
- Parliament Buildings
- Te Papa
- Cable-car
- Martinborough wine region

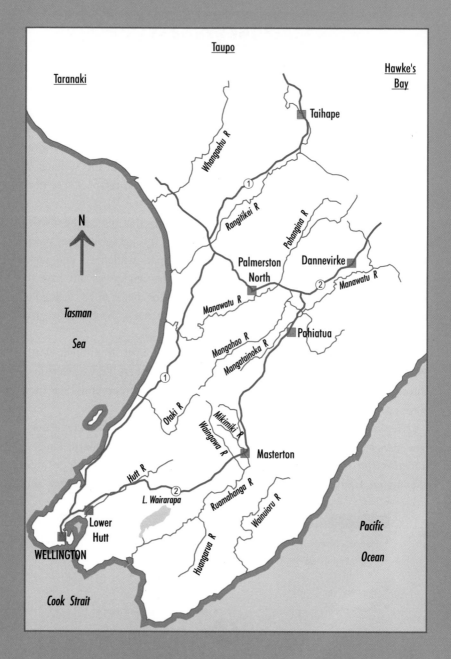

excite experienced anglers. While the 241 km-long Rangitikei River – the most extensive single fishery in the region – shares with the Awakino, north of New Plymouth, the distinction of holding sea-run brown trout.

Complementing the fishing is a fine range of dining options and places to stay. The Martinborough district in the Wairarapa is becoming increasingly known for the quality of its wineries, and Wellington City has become the tourism benchmark by which other cities must be judged. People-friendly downtown redevelopment enhances an already picturesque harbour. Wellington claims to have more cafés per head of population than any other city in the country. It also has more politicians . . .

INFORMATION

Fish and Game New Zealand
Wellington region
188 Broadway Ave
PO Box 1325
Palmerston North
06 359 0409
www.fishandgame.org.nz
Manager: Peter Hill
Field Officers: Peter Taylor; Miranda Robinson

Wellington office
1st Floor, 2 Jarden Mile
Ngaraunga
PO Box 9518, Te Aro
Wellington
04 477 6118
Field Officer: Blake Abernethy

Wellington Flyfishers Club
PO Box 9236
Te Aro
Wellington

Wellington Visitor Information Centre
cnr Wakefield Street and Civic Square
Wellington
04 802 4860
www.wellingtonnz.com

Upper Hutt Visitor Information Centre
6 Main Street
Upper Hutt
04 527 2141
uhvic@uhcc.govt.nz
www.upperhuttcity.com

Kapiti Coast Visitor Information Centre
Centennial Park
SH1 Otaki
06 364 7620
kapiti.info@clear.net.nz
www.kcdc.govt.nz

Masterton Visitor Information Centre
5 Dixon Street
Masterton
06 378 7373
info@wairarapanz.com
www.wairarapanz.com

Martinborough Visitor Information Centre
18 Kitchener Street
Martinborough
06 306 9043
martinborough@wairarapanz.com

i

WHERE AND WHAT

The Fish and Game New Zealand Wellington region includes all of the southern portion of the North Island with a skewed northern boundary that at its centre reaches north to Waiouru into the southern Kaimanawa Ranges.

The region has four major fishing rivers – the Rangitikei, Manawatu, Ruamahunga and Hutt – and is split north and south by the Kaimanawa, Ruahine and Tararua Forest Parks where lie ideal waters for wilderness/back-country fishing.

All the rivers and streams hold brown trout, and rainbows are found in a few. Most waters are open all year and have no bag limit. A few waters have a very low bag limit and some are managed as trophy fisheries and so have a maximum size limit. Access to most rivers and streams is public and readily available, but the river and stream margins are often over private land and landowner permission is needed to traverse along them. Fish and Game Wellington region has a series of pamphlets with a colour map showing access points. These are usually available at tackle shops.

The Wellington region fishing regulations follow the general North Island regulations. Waters in the region open all year are all coastal dune lakes: Moawhango River; Hokowhitu Lagoon; Ohau River; Hutt River; Oroua River, downstream of the Ruahine Forest Park boundary; Kawhatau River; Otaki River, downstream of the Tararua Forest Park boundary; Henley Lake; Pohangina River; Lake Wairarapa; Porirua Lakes; Makakahi River, downstream from the road bridge at Eketahuna; Manawatu River, downstream from its confluence with the Mangatewainui Stream; Mangahao River, downstream from

Marima Reserve bridge; Mangaone River; Mangatainoka River, downstream from the junction with the Makakahi River; Rangitikei River, downstream from the Matawhero Road bridge; Ruamahunga River, downstream of the Tararua Forest Park boundary; Tauherenikau River, downstream of the Tararua Forest Park boundary; Tiraumea River; Upper Kourarau Dam; Waingawa River, downstream of the Tararura Forest Park boundary; Waiohine River, downstream of the Tararua Forest Park boundary; Whitby Lakes. All other waters in the region are closed from 30 April to 1 October.

On the Rangitikei River upstream of the Matawhero Road bridge there is a daily bag limit of four trout but they must be no longer than 55 cm. On the Hautapu and Wainuiomata Rivers there are fly fishing only restrictions and a daily bag limit of one trout that must be no longer than 55 cm. Fly fishing only restrictions also apply to the Kopuaranga, Mangatoro, Mangatarere and Makuri Streams.

A daily bag limit of one trout applies to the Akatarawa River; Hutt River; Mangaohane Stream; Mangatarere Stream; Makuri River; Manawatu River, upstream of its confluence with the Mangatewainui Stream; Pakuratahi Stream; Pourangaki River; Rangitikei River, upstream of the confluence of Otarere Stream; Tokomaru River; Upper Kourarau Dam; Waikanae River; Wainuiomata River; Whakatikei River; and all waters upstream of the boundaries of the Ruahine, Tararua and Rimutaka Forest Parks. Trout taken from the Akatarawa River, Hutt River, Pakuratahi River, Pourangaki River, Tokomaru River and Whakatikei River must be smaller than 45 cm.

Casting  around

Manawatu River

The Manawatu River has its source east of the Ruahine Range yet empties
into the Tasman Sea west of the ranges. Its 170 km of fishable water flow in
a south-westerly direction beginning north of Dannevirke, past Woodville,
Ashhurst, Palmerston North and Foxton. Access is readily available from a
number of roads either paralleling or leading to the river over most of its
length. Almost all of the fishing is done between Dannevirke and Palmerston
North. Fishing conditions vary as the river changes from a very small gravel
bed channel meandering past papa cliffs to the expansive, slow-flowing and
often turbid waters of the lower river. Throughout its length brown trout is
the mainstay of this fishery although rainbow trout are becoming more
numerous. The fishing can become difficult in summer when water levels
fall. Throughout the season, dawn excursions often find trout cruising in the
shallows. Fish usually need to be stalked.

Mangatainoka River

With its source in the eastern Tararua Range, the Mangatainoka River
parallels SH2 flowing toward Pahiatua and has about 50 km of fishable
water with numerous roads leading to the river off the state highway.
Numerous bridges give easy access to most of the river. The upper reaches at
Putara are excellent early in the season with clear, deep pools and boulder
runs. When the water warms most of the trout drop back downstream. The
middle and lower reaches are mostly willow-lined, similar in character, with
long pools and glides interspersed with shallow riffles.

Makuri River

The Makuri River, a tributary of the Tiraumea River, is east of Pahiatua and
flows in a westerly direction. Access is initially off SH2 onto the
Pahiatua/Akitio/Pongaroa Road. A challenging small river rising in the
limestone country of the Puketoi Ranges, the Makuri is the closest to a chalk

stream in the region. The most easily accessible fishing is above the gorge upstream of the Makuri township. Downstream the river flows through a rugged gorge of huge boulders and fast, tumbling waters – access is difficult. Morning is regarded as the best time to be on the Makuri.

Tiraumea River

The source of the Tiraumea River is in the sandstone/mudstone hill country east of Pahiatua and flows in a northerly direction to join the Manawatu River near Woodville. Access is initially off SH2 at Mangatainoka or Pahiatua. The least well-known of the rivers in the Pahiatua region, the Tiraumea is not heavily fished. The fish have a tendency to cruise, making a careful approach to sighted fish with dry fly or an unweighted caddis nymph the favoured method. Access is not easy because of steep-sided stream banks that are often heavily vegetated.

Mangahao River

The Mangahao flows from the eastern flank of the Tararua Range in a north-easterly direction towards Woodville. Access from Palmerston North or Pahiatua (SH2) is off the Pahiatua Track Road. It is an attractive river to fish, although being comparatively steep its highly varied flow produces inconsistent numbers of fish. The best fishing is early in the season and a mild stable winter seems to encourage fish to remain in the river.

Makakahi River

The Makakahi River drains from the eastern Tararua Range and flows towards Pahiatua; it parallels SH2 and is accessible off this highway for all of its length. Most fishing is focused on the 30 km or so between Eketahuna and its confluence with the Mangatainoka River. Upstream of this point the fishing tends to be patchy, with the early season favoured.

Pohangina River

The Pohangina River has its source on the western flank of the Ruahine Range and flows south to join the Manawatu River at Ashhurst. Access is initially off SH3 onto Pohangina Road and then either Pohangina Road East or Pohangina Road West, which parallel the river for about 40 km. It is a relatively unstable river in a wide channel with extensive gravel beaches. There are good trout numbers along its length although they fluctuate depending on the frequency and severity of flooding.

Kahuterawa Stream

A picturesque small stream near Palmerston North, the small pools and bubbling rapids can provide an enjoyable day's fishing. Access is off Old West Road behind Massey University.

Tokomaru River

The Tokomaru rises on the western side of the Tararua Range and flows west to cross SH57, between Palmerston North and Shannon. The headwaters provide mountain-style fishing in high-quality surroundings for good-sized but few fish. It is a rugged area with deep pools and numerous large boulders making progress very difficult in places and is only recommended for fit anglers.

Oroua River

The Oroua exits the western Ruahine Range at Apiti to flow south through Feilding. There is reasonable access into the ranges off the end of Table Flat Road and, for the moderately fit angler, the fishing is very enjoyable in scenic and peaceful surroundings although trout numbers are generally low.

Rangitikei River

The Rangitikei River has its source in the Kaimanawa Ranges, east of Lake Taupo and flows southward to the Tasman Sea

TACKLE BOX

Upper Hutt Gun Shop
29A Montgomery Crescent
Upper Hutt
Wellington
04 939 6184

The Tackle Shop
102 Kapiti Road
Paraparaumu
04 902 9977

The Sports Spot
86–90 Vivian Street
Wellington
04 381 0205

Wellington Hunting and Fishing
444 Cuba Street
Lower Hutt
04 589 9500

The Sports Cave
49 Ghuznee Street
Wellington
04 384 5105

Stirling Sports
44 Willis Street
Wellington
04 472 8108

about 50 km below Wanganui. Most of its 241 km length provides good to excellent fishing ranging from trophy rainbow and brown trout in wilderness surroundings to estuary-dwelling sea-runs. Access to the headwaters is best by helicopter although for the very fit angler there is a track leading off the Desert Road. The many kilometres of accessible middle and lower reaches are the most popular, with year-round fishing available from many roads leading off SH1.

GUIDES AND CHARTERS

David Webb
143 Oxford Street
Ashhurst
06 326 8423
davidweb@man.quik.co.nz
www.man.quik.co.nz/davidweb/

Hautapu River

The headwaters of the Hautapu River are in comparatively unmodified low, rolling tussock country east of Waiouru and not from a mountain range. It is a comparatively small waterway and contains good numbers of relatively large brown trout and is managed as a 'trophy' fishery. Access is mostly off SH1, which tends to follow the river, and angler access along the majority of the river is public although this is erratic.

Whakaurekou River

This river joins the Rangitikei east of Taihape after running off the steep slopes of the western Ruahine Range. Access is either via the Rangitikei River walking upstream from Mokai off the end of Mokai Road (landowner permission is required and the river must be low), or via private farm access off Pukeokahu Road opposite the confluence with the Rangitikei. However, fish numbers can vary greatly from year to year. It is one of the most scenic small-river fisheries in the district. Best fished early or late in the season.

HOROWHENUA–KAPITI COAST DISTRICT

This district's rivers are unusual in the sense that they run from the Tararua Range over a short distance to the Tasman Sea. There is not a major river fishery parenting several smaller rivers, as is the case for our other districts. As a consequence, fishing can be variable as floods have a significant impact on trout recruitment. Nonetheless, there are three moderately popular fisheries in the district that invite fishing time.

Waikanae River

This fishery offers a diverse and rewarding angling experience, particularly to the fly fisher. It is a small river, short, and takes anglers through a back-country to estuary fishing experience all within the space of 15 km. Access is off SH1. The river holds moderate numbers of good-condition brown trout with the best fishing in the middle and lower reaches.

Otaki River

The Otaki, a medium-sized river, has an extensive catchment within the Tararua Forest Park, and after leaving the Tararua Range runs a rapid course to the sea. It is a highly variable fishery with floods regularly turning over a relatively unstable bed. Access to the Forest Park is off SH1 via Otaki Gorge Road, which follows the south bank of the river. Walking access from the road end can take up to several days and anglers need to be fit and well-equipped for mountain fishing.

Ohau River

A small river where the fishing improves as you go further downstream. Vulnerable to the impact of floods, again fish numbers vary greatly. Access is off SH1, and to go upstream take either Muhunoa East Road, Kimberley Road or, to the Forest Park, Tararua and Gladstone Roads.

WELLINGTON DISTRICT

There is a surprising array of trout-fishing opportunities around the capital city of New Zealand. In fact, there is probably no other major city in the world with a quality brown trout fishery so close at hand.

Hutt River

The Hutt, largest of the Wellington rivers, dominates angling interest. Access is easy with riverside parks or access tracks along most of its length. In general, anglers' fish 'blind' and cover the water rather than sight-fish.

Spinning or wet fly fishing is also popular. The time for spinning is either early season (particularly if the water is slightly discoloured) or late in the season when trout become aggressive leading up to spawning. A small wet fly drifted across the tail of the pool is a favoured method during summer. Mornings or evenings are prime times in the summer. A sinking line is best after dark.

Wainuiomata River

The Wainuiomata rises in the Rimutaka Range to flow south to the township of Wainuiomata and then out some 20 km to the sea. Access is off the Wainuiomata Coast Road and landowner permission is required. Dissimilar in nature to all other rivers in the Wellington area, this river, managed as a 'trophy' brown trout fishery, provides a real challenge to anglers. Slow-flowing, with high banks and little streamside vegetation, cruising trout are easy to spot but difficult to catch. Most nymph patterns work and fish will take a dry fly throughout the season, mainly on warm days and in the evening. A wet fly can be effective when fished in the surface film during the hatch. Most of the best fishing is in the middle to lower reaches.

Akatarawa River

One of three 'mountain stream'-type rivers, it is a clear, swift-flowing river carrying a moderate number of fish, especially earlier in the summer. The narrow Akatarawa Valley confines the river to a restricted channel, with tight rock-walled gorges restricting access for anglers at several points. The highest fish populations occur in the two open areas of the valley at Karapoti Road and Cloustonville. These reaches have a high proportion of boulder-run habitat that provides excellent fly fishing. In the main, this is a lower-density trout fishery. The clear waters assist fish spotting and usually anglers fish to sighted fish.

Pakuratahi River

This river has its headwaters in the Rimutaka Range, and flows north under SH2 to join the Hutt River at Kaitoke. Access on the Rimutaka side is from the Rimutaka Incline Walkway; a foot track follows the river for a number of kilometres. The river is confined within a narrow valley and there are regular

HANG YOUR HOOK

Whispering Pines
207 Colletts Road
RD1 Mangaroa
Upper Hutt
04 526 7785
whisperingpines@xtra.co.nz
a country welcome in the Mangaroa Valley

Terracotta Lodge
6 Rutland Road
Carterton
06 379 5583
ronaldvkeene@xtra.co.nz
www.wairarapa.co.nz/terracottalodge
luxury homestay with all meals

Fresh Egg Retreat
Bute Road
RD9 Masterton
Wairarapa
06 372 3506
hosts@freshegg.co.nz
home cooking in a secluded retreat

The Ambers
78 Kuratawhiti Street
Greytown
Wairarapa
06 304 8588
ambershomestay@xtra.co.nz
boutique bed and breakfast in restored colonial home

The Martinborough Hotel
The Square
Martinborough
06 306 9350
info@martinboroughhotel.co.nz
www.martinboroughhotel.co.nz
historic boutique hotel in the heart of Martinborough wine village

McLeods
White Rock Road
Hautotara
RD2 Martinborough
06 306 9032
trout fishing in three rivers on the 520 ha Mcleods farm

Tarata Homestead
5251 Mokai Road
RD3 Taihape
06 388 0354
a river full of trout runs through this remote Rangitikei River homestay

Plaisted Park Homestay
11 Feltham Street
Hunterville
Rangitikei
06 322 8215
peaceful homestay close to the township

Fernside Lodge
Fernside
RD1 Featherston
Fernside.lodge@xtra.co.nz
www.fernside.co.nz
classic luxury down to the chauffeured vintage car

Wharekaukau Country Estate
Western Lake Road
Palliser Bay
06 307 77581
wharekauhau.lodge@xtra.co.nz
top-shelf luxury lodge with an international reputation

Koeke Lodge
Upper Plain Road
Masterton
06 377 2414
koekelodge@xtra.co.nz
surrounded by lavender gardens

deep pools where the water flow cuts in against rock bluffs. Fish are few but relatively easy to spot in the clear water in peaceful, attractive surroundings.

Mangaroa River

The Mangaroa has its headwaters on the western flank of the Rimutaka Range immediately above Upper Hutt. Apart from the first 2 km upstream of the mouth to Maymorn there is no public access – landowner permission is required to get access to and along the river. Renowned for its free-rising trout, the Mangaroa fishes best early in the season when a number of Hutt River spawners are still loitering before returning to the Hutt. Trout rise freely during the evening and can be taken on most general fly patterns.

Whakatiki River

The Whakatiki, across the Hutt River from Upper Hutt, is a quality mountain-stream fishery. Access is either by crossing the Hutt River at the confluence off SH2, giving reasonable fishing for about 1 km before entering a tight gorge, or via Moonshine and Bull Run Roads. A locked gate stops vehicle access directly to the Whakatiki but it is only a walk of several hundred metres along the Wainui Stream to reach it. While carrying only moderate numbers of trout, the impressive surroundings, deep clear pools and bubbling runs bordered by steep bush-covered slopes amply reward the adventurous angler who is prepared to walk a bit for their fishing.

CATCH A MEAL

The Martinborough Hotel
The Square
Martinborough
06 306 9350
info@martinboroughhotel.co.nz
www.martinboroughhotel.co.nz
classic country cuisine

Salute!
83 Main Street
Greytown
06 304 9825
eve_travis@yahoo.com
modern Mediterranean cuisine

Zibibbo
25–29 Taranaki Street
Wellington
04 385 6650
dine@zibibbo.co.nz
contemporary Spanish and Italian

Theo's Greek Taverna
13 Pirie Street
Mt Victoria
Wellington
04 801 8806
fun@theosgreektaverna.co.nz
www.theosgreektaverna.co.nz
New Zealand's best Greek restaurant

Blue Island Seafoods
131 Randwick Road
Moera
Lower Hutt
04 568 2806
the country's best fish-and-chip shop in 2000

CATCH A MEAL

The Black Stump
173 Main Street
Pahiatua
06 376 7123
steak and pasta in an old barn

Chocolate Fish Café
497A Karaka Bay Road
Scorching Bay
Wellington
04 388 2808
lunch on panini and watch the seals

Boulcott Street Bistro
99 Boulcott Street
Wellington
04 499 4199
www.boulcott.com
first in first served

Fishermans Table
Oriental Bay
Wellington
04 801 7900
www.fishermanstable.co.nz
seafood with the harbour at your feet

WELLINGTON'S SMALL STREAMS

Small streams abound in the rugged Wellington landscape. Waters such as the Makara (access is either through Karori to the middle reaches at Makara or Ohariu to the lower reaches), Korokoro (off SH2 opposite Petone), and Pauatahanui (access off SH2 over Haywards Hill or via Paremata to Pauatahanui), provide interesting fishing attracting a small number of anglers. Don't expect large fish and numbers can vary from year to year. Early season is better.

WAIRARAPA DISTRICT

River trolling, a rarity in trout fishing, is popular on the lower reaches of the Ruamahanga River in the Wairarapa. Henley Lake is the best small-lake fishery in the region for children. For all its quality, fishing pressure is generally light and you are unlikely to see another angler during a day's fishing.

Ruamahanga River

The Ruamahanga River rises in the Tararua Range and drains southward over 120 km past Masterton to enter the sea at Lake Ferry. Access to the river is quite good. The upper Ruamahanga within the Tararua Forest Park has walking access either at Mt Bruce, where SH2 crosses the river, or via the headwaters of the Mangatainoka River at Putara. The river here is classic wilderness fishing with a comparatively small number of large fish in gin-clear water. Best fished midsummer when wading conditions are comfortable and trout are actively feeding.

Downstream of Martinborough access can be gained from either side of the river off either Kahutara Road or the Martinborough–Lake Ferry Road, where the river is bigger and has numerous large pools with high numbers of fish. Fly fishing is favoured during summer as temperatures rise and hatches of natural fly become prolific. Further downstream below the Tuhitarata Bridge, trolling is popular especially in the autumn when sea-run brown trout move into the river.

Kopuaranga River

This small river, with its origins in the hill country to the north of Masterton, is the only one of its kind in the Wairarapa. There is no public access along this river – landowner permission is required. A small meandering stream frequently overhung by willows, the Kopuaranga, a fly fishing only stream, holds good numbers of fish and is a favourite of fly fishers.

Waipoua River

The Waipoua River originates in the eastern foothills of the Tararua Range and flows southward to join the Ruamahanga River at Masterton. The river parallels SH2 and access is possible off a number of roads off Paierau Road or SH2. An important spawning tributary of the Ruamahanga, this river holds a limited population of resident fish year-round.

Tauweru River

The Tauweru River has an extensive catchment to the east of Masterton and joins the Ruamahanga at Gladstone. The river is slow-flowing and willow-lined and is best suited to anglers who like to stalk cruising fish. There is excellent fishing in the lower 3 km of this river and it generally fishes best when the willow grub is prevalent during the summer months.

Waiohine River

This large tributary of the Ruamahunga River flows from the eastern side of the Tararua Range and can provide excellent wilderness fishing in the upper reaches for the fit angler. Accesses to the middle and lower reaches are off a number of roads that parallel the river upstream or downstream of SH2. Fishing is fair to good in these reaches depending on the frequency and severity of flood flows. Fly fishing is the favoured method. Access to the Tararua Forest Park is by the Waiohine Gorge Road to Walls Whare and walking from there. Alternatively, a climb up and over Mt Holdsworth from the Mt Holdsworth Road will get a very fit angler into the mid Waiohine Hut. Upstream of Totara Flats it is recommended only for the very fit angler.

Waingawa River

This medium-sized tributary of the Ruamahanga River flows from the eastern side of the Tararua Range. It can provide excellent wilderness fishing in the upper reaches for the fit angler where the river is managed as a trophy fishery although fish are not numerous. Access is off Upper Plain Road to Upper Waingawa Road and then walking from the road end; it is very scenic within the Tararua Forest Park. Downstream of the park fish are scarce. Summer offers the best fishing when wading is easier because of lower river

WHEN THE FISH DON'T BITE

Adventure Centre
76 Main Road
Greytown
06 304 8565
info@ecoadventure.co.nz
www.ecoadventure.co.nz
kayak and raft the Waiohine Gorge

Martinborough Wet 'n' Wild
3 Kitchener Street
Martinborough
06 306 8252
martinboroughwetnwild@xtra.co.nz
jet-boat the Ruamahanga River

The Horse and Carriage Establishment
RD1 Clareville
Carterton
06 379 6494
jsig@wise.net.nz
Martinborough wine trail by pony and trap

Te Papa
Cable Street
Wellington
04 381 7000
mail@tepapa.govt.nz
www.tepapa.govt.nz
more than a museum; admission free

Fly by Wire
BP Service Station
State Highway 1
Paekakariki
0800 359 299
fly@flybywire.co.nz
www.flybywire.co.nz
like flying a fighter plane?

Ballooning New Zealand
54B Kent Street
Carterton
06 379 8223
hot-air ballooning

levels and warmer temperatures. Fish a large weighted nymph to sighted fish or try a large deer hair dry fly if cicadas are abundant. Fly fishing is the best method.

Tauherenikau River

This medium-sized river flows from the eastern side of the Tararua Range into Lake Wairarapa just north of Featherston. Access to the Forest Park is either from Underhill Road and Bucks Road (from Featherston or Greytown), or from the Upper Hutt side of the Rimutaka Range at Kaitoke and walking three hours from the car park off Marchant Road. The upper reaches in the park provide good wilderness angling.

Henley Lake

A smallish, man-made lake near the centre of Masterton, Henley Lake is stocked annually with rainbow trout and is an ideal area for junior anglers to fish safely and for families to picnic while fishing together.

Kourarau Dam

The Kourarau dam is a water-supply lake that has been a popular fishing spot for many years. Access is at Gladstone immediately south of Masterton off the Martinborough–Masterton Road then off Tupurupuru–Te Wharau Road. The dam holds impressive-sized rainbow trout. It is managed as a 'trophy' rainbow lake fishery – the only one of its type in the Wellington region.

Nelson/
Marlborough

New Zealand is often said to contain a little of most other countries in the world. And if you had to choose a region in New Zealand that contains a bit of everything found elsewhere in the country, there would be none to surpass Nelson/Marlborough. It has mountains that are snowcapped for six months of the year, beaches of tropically golden sand where fur seals loll offshore, virgin native forests, deeply indented sounds, high-country plateaus, rugged coastlines, and a climate in which the annual sunshine hours are consistently the highest in New Zealand. Small as the region is, it also contains three national parks and a maritime park – including the Abel Tasman National Park, which draws visitors from all over the world.

To complement these abundant gifts of nature – and perhaps because of them – the Nelson/Marlborough region has fostered two distinctive products of man. One is an arts and crafts scene that is more dense and vibrant than anywhere else in the country – in Nelson alone there are more than 300 full-time artists working in a variety of different media – and the other is a wine industry which has achieved international recognition, particularly for its sauvignon blanc. The vineyards are situated mainly on the stony, alluvial flats created by rivers that carry huge volumes of gravel in their tumbling waters.

FAMOUS FOR

- Marlborough Sounds
- sauvignon blanc wines
- Nelson Lakes National Park
- Molesworth Station
- Mt Tapuae o Uenuku
- Queen Charlotte Track
- Abel Tasman National Park
- sunshine
- arts and crafts
- Lord Rutherford

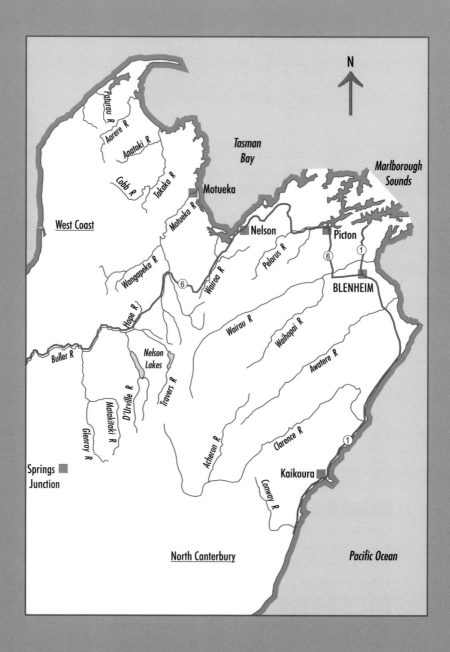

Those same rivers also contain handsome numbers of wild brown trout. Browns thrive in Nelson/Marlborough and there are few waters in the region that cannot sustain them; many rivers hold sea-run brown trout too. Rainbow trout have not fared so well, although they are found in some lakes and reservoirs. So for a near perfect mix of wine, food, culture, outdoor adventure, magnificent climate – and brown trout in abundance – it would be hard to find a more inviting region than Nelson/Marlborough.

INFORMATION

Fish and Game New Zealand
Nelson/Marlborough region
66 Champion Road
Richmond
Nelson
PO Box 2173
Stoke
Nelson
03 544 6382
ndeans@nmfgc.co.nz
www.fishandgame.org.nz
Manager: Neil Deans
Field Officers: Lawson Davey (Nelson)
David Oberdries (Blenheim)
03 578 8421

Destination Marlborough
Blenheim
03 577 5523
Dest.Marlborough@xtra.co.nz
www.destinationmarlborough.com

Tourism Nelson
cnr of Trafalgar and Halifax Streets
PO Box 788
Nelson
03 546 6228
info@tourism-nelson.co.nz
www.nelson.net.nz

Nelson Visitor Information Centre
cnr Trafalgar and Halifax Streets
Nelson
03 548 2304

Motueka Visitor Information Centre
Wallace Street
Motueka
03 528 6543

Marlborough Freshwater Anglers Club
Roger Winter
03 578 3473
roger@theoldtrout.com

Motueka Freshwater Anglers Club
John Craze
03 528 8309
Ralph Dixon
03 528 9232

River flow information
Tasman District Council
03 544 3393
www.tdc.govt.nz

Marborough District Council
03 577 2541
www.marlborough.govt.nz

WHERE AND WHAT

The Nelson/Marlborough region stretches from Kahurangi Point in the north-west, south to Springs Junction, and east to the Conway River catchment near Kaikoura. It contains three National Parks, one Forest Park, the Marlborough Sounds Maritime Park, more than 20 water catchments and several lakes. Some 40 per cent of the region is within the Department of Conservation estate. The climate is diverse and so is the landscape – which has a significant impact on the region's rivers and fishing quality.

After rain, rivers in Golden Bay soon turn dark brown from tannin leaching out of the bush catchments. However, those flowing out of the Waimea basin's upper catchments, such as the Wairoa, Upper Motueka, Wangapeka, Baton and Pearce, are noted for their water clarity. The Murchison district offers everything from small feeder streams to the impressive Buller River, New Zealand's fifth largest – in flood, it rises more than 30 vertical metres at Hawks Crag near Westport. The Buller is fed by the snowmelt waters of Lakes Rotoiti and Rotoroa, until it is joined by the Matakitaki, Mangles, Matiri and Maruia near Murchison.

Most Marlborough rivers, in contrast to those in Nelson, are blue with glacial silt, wide, braided and with extremes of flow. The Clarence River, which drains the Kaikoura Ranges, and the Awatere, are heavily silt-laden for much of the year. The Wairau River is one of the area's best trout fisheries, producing large sea-run and resident fish. In the Marlborough Sounds' main catchment, the Pelorus Valley, the river gouges its way through steep native bush-covered mountains, slowing to a gentle pace in lush dairy-farm land before entering the sea at Havelock.

The Nelson/Marlborough region's regulations follow the general South Island regulations. There is a closed season from 30 April to 1 October on the upper reaches of most rivers and streams, but the downstream sections, and the lakes and reservoirs in the region, are mostly open to fishing year-round, including the Aorere River – downstream from the road bridge at Rockville; Argyle Pond and lower hydro canals – downstream to its confluence with the Wairau River; Awatere River; Buller River – downstream from Gowan Bridge; Clarence River – downstream from the Acheron confluence; Cobb Reservoir; Conway River; Lake Rotoiti; Lake Rotoroa; Lyell Creek (Kaikoura) – downstream from SH1; Maitai River – below the Lower Nile Street Bridge; Maruia River – downstream of Maruia Falls; Matakitaki River – downstream from the SH6 Bridge; Middle Creek (Kaikoura) – downstream from SH1; Motueka River – downstream from the road bridge at Ngatimoti; Oaro River; Opawa River – downstream from the SH1 Bridge, including Roses Overflow; Pelorus River – downstream from its confluence with the Rai River; Takaka River – downstream from its confluence with the Waingaro River; Taylor River – downstream from the New Renwick Road Bridge; Waimea or Wairoa Rivers – downstream of the Lee River confluence; Wairau River (including the Diversion) – downstream from the Wash Bridge.

The daily bag limit on the region's rivers and streams is two trout, but in most headwaters and smaller tributary fisheries where adult trout numbers are low, only one fish can be longer than 50 cm – these waters include Branch River; Daniell's Lake; Deepdale River; D'Urville River; Glenroy River; Goulter

River; Matakitaki River – upstream of its confluence with the Glenroy River; Motueka River – upstream of its confluence with the Wangapeka River; Motupiko River; Opouri River; Owen River; Pearse River; Pelorus River – upstream of its confluence with the Rai River; Rahu River; Rainbow River; Riwaka River; Ronga River; Sabine River; Spring Creek; Travers River; Warwick River; Whakapuaka River; Woolley River. The restriction is intended to maintain breeding stocks. Elsewhere, there is no minimum size limit for trout.

Fish & Game New Zealand's Nelson/Marlborough region has an excellent series of maps detailing access points and fishing regulations in each of the major catchments. These are available from the Fish and Game regional office or at most tackle shops.

TACKLE BOX

Picton Sports & Outdoors
8 High Street
Picton
03 573 6963

Coppins Great Outdoors Centre
255 High Street
Motueka
Nelson
03 528 7296

Stirling Sports
83 Market Street
Blenheim
03 578 8017

Mitchell Sportsworld
10 Wynen Street
Blenheim
03 578 4421

Motueka Sports World
201 High Street
Motueka
03 528 9845

Rollo's Great Outdoors Centre
12 Bridge Street
Nelson
03 548 1975

Sportsworld Richmond
213 Queen Street
Richmond
Nelson
03 544 8290

Nelson Sports World
83 Bridge Street
Nelson
03 548 1708

Nelson Hunting & Fishing
Montgomery Square Car Park
Nelson
03 548 1840

Big Blue Dive & Fish
cnr Akerston Street and Wildman Ave
Nelson
03 546 7411

Stirling Sports
247 Trafalgar Street
Nelson
03 548 3974

Casting 🎣 around

AORERE RIVER AND ITS TRIBUTARIES

The Aorere River is the largest in Golden Bay and offers many kilometres of back-country fishing for large brown trout in scenic surroundings. The water is often a brownish colour but in the upper reaches is extremely clear and deep. The upper river is part of the Tasman Wilderness section of the Kahurangi National Park. Here the going is difficult, but the keen angler is often rewarded with large and challenging fish. The main river features several impressive gorges with accessible reaches between them. The lower river provides productive angling for sea-run trout and kahawai.

AWATERE RIVER AND ITS TRIBUTARIES

The Awatere River tends to be ignored because of its extreme flows and poor clarity. Yet when it is clear, local spin anglers catch some nice trout – mainly at the mouth or middle to upper sections of pools. Fly fishers find some interesting sport in the larger side-streams.

BULLER RIVER AND ITS TRIBUTARIES

This fishery is important enough to warrant a National Water Conservation Order and attracts many anglers. Access to most reaches is easy, with roads close by and agreeable landowners who grant access permission upon request. The Buller and tributaries give the angler many choices of fishing location and trout size, numbers and catchability. All angling methods work, with fly fishing being the most productive in clear water.

CLARENCE RIVER AND ITS TRIBUTARIES

The lower and middle sections of the Clarence are silt-laden for much of the year, but do clear at times in the summer or midwinter. Most angling is from the Acheron River confluence upstream, where there is good road access.

This section of river is often clear and holds plenty of small- to medium-sized trout that love dry flies and spinners.

Lake Tennyson holds good numbers of medium-sized trout, with high numbers of small trout in the first 2 km of the Clarence River below the lake's outlet. The Acheron River and its tributaries hold larger trout with many kilometres of rivers to explore. Foot access is available all summer and vehicle access along the Acheron only when the road through Molesworth Station is open to the public in December and January.

MOTUEKA RIVER AND ITS TRIBUTARIES

This is the region's most popular fishing river and also has a National Water Conservation Order pending. It is only one hour's drive from Nelson and has an abundance of easy access to the main river and all tributaries. It also supports one of New Zealand's highest trout populations, with excellent angling opportunities for resident and sea-run brown trout up to 2 kg. Fish twice that size are found throughout its length. Trout numbers in the Motueka have declined slightly in recent years, but as a result trout size has increased. All angling methods can be used successfully. Many of the feeder streams – such as the Pearse, Dove, Tadmor and Rainy – offer good fishing. The Wangapeka and Baton also hold good-sized trout, but in low numbers.

NELSON LAKES NATIONAL PARK

Lakes Rotoiti, Rotoroa and the Travers, Sabine and D'Urville Rivers provide superb wilderness fishing. DoC has built

GUIDES AND CHARTERS

Clearwater Trout Guides
c/o Fisherman's Rest
Waiwhero Road
RD1 Motueka
03 526 8086

John Brunwin
97 Murphy Street
Nelson
03 548 9145
trout@tasman.net

Peter Carty
Chalgrave Street
Murchison
03 523 9525
p.carty@xtra.co.nz
www.BrownTroutHeaven.co.nz

Boris Cech
RD2 Rotoiti
Nelson
03 521 1840
kehu.guiding@clear.net.nz

good tracks, bridges and huts that anglers can use, as well as water taxi services on both lakes. Trout numbers are good, with fly fishing being the most productive in the clear waters. Trolling sometimes works well on these lakes.

PELORUS RIVER AND ITS TRIBUTARIES

The Pelorus is a beautiful river with wild rugged headwaters and gentle lowland reaches. About 70 per cent of its trout are browns – some more than 3 kg – with the rest rainbows of around 1 kg. The river is an excellent choice for the less experienced angler and for winter angling, and is well served by DoC huts and tracks. The catchment has several rivers, such as the Rai and Wakamarina, and their tributary streams, that are worth exploring with a fly rod.

GUIDES AND CHARTERS

Tony Entwistle
5 Mason Place
Richmond
Nelson
03 544 4565
enty@internet.co.nz

Peter Flintoft
18 Hampden Street
Murchison
03 523 9315

Ron McKay
31 Hotham Street
Murchison
03 523 9533

Graeme Marshall
Waiwhero Road
Ngatimoto
RD1 Motueka
03 526 8800
marshall@tasman.net
www.BrownTroutHeaven.co.nz

TAKAKA RIVER AND ITS TRIBUTARIES

A popular Golden Bay river with unusual flow patterns caused by variable flows from an upstream power station and water flowing underground to feed the Pupu Springs, the largest and clearest in the Southern Hemisphere. The Cobb Reservoir in the headwaters holds lots of small rainbows and some browns. The upper Takaka is rugged but well serviced with the hydro road, and this section and major tributaries – the Anatoki and Waingaro – hold low numbers of good strong brown trout. The section of the Takaka River from Lindsay's Bridge to the Waingaro confluence is often dry. Pupu Springs are always clear and hold huge brown trout.

HANG YOUR HOOK

Raetihi Lodge
Kenepuru Road
Double Bay
Kenepuru Sound
03 573 4300
hotel@raetihi.co.nz
www.raetihi.co.nz
can be reached by water taxi

Craglee Lodge
Bay of Many Coves
Queen Charlotte Sound
03 579 9223
craglee@xtra.co.nz
perched above the bay in the heart of the Marlborough Sounds

The Old St Mary's Convent
Rapaura Road
RD3 Blenheim
03 570 5700
oldstmary@xtra.co.nz
www.nz.com/travel/old.st.marys
elegant lodge built in 1890 for the Sisters of Mercy and restored under the direction of Sir Michael Fowler

The Peppertree
900 State Highway 1
Riverlands
Blenheim
03 520 9200
thepeppertree@xtra.co.nz
luxury accommodation in a restored farmhouse

Muritai Manor
48 Wakapuaka Road
Wakapuaka
RD1 Nelson
muritai.manor@xtra.co.nz
www.Muritai.Manor.webnz.co.nz
Edwardian manor with views across Tasman Bay to Abel Tasman National Park

Cambria House
7 Cambria Street
Nelson
03 548 4681
cambria@clear.net.nz
simple, but inviting with delightful cuisine

The Baywick Inn
51 Domett Street
Nelson
03 545 6514
baywicks@iconz.co.nz
restored Victorian villa overlooking the Maitai River and bordering Brook Stream

The Honest Lawyer
1 Point Road
Monaco
Nelson
03 547 8850
thl@ts.co.nz
Waimea estuary pub honoured by the Hospitality Association for outstanding customer service

Mapledurham
8 Edward Street
Richmond
Nelson
03 544 4210
mapledurham@ts.co.nz
historic ambience, superb hospitality and award-winning restaurants close by

Bronte Lodge
Bronte Road East
Upper Moutere
RD1 Nelson
03 540 2422
margaret@brontelodge.co.nz
pathways lead to the shores of the Waimea estuary

WAIMEA RIVER AND ITS TRIBUTARIES

Nelson anglers like the Waimea because it is close to town – and because its clear waters are ideal for stalking large resident and sea-run trout. The lower section is modified to control floods but still produces large fish, the upper reaches and tributaries are gorgy in places with most trout more than 2 kg, in top condition, and exciting to catch. River levels rise quickly in heavy rain but fall and clear just as quickly. During a hot summer with low flows, fishing can be best at night. Fishing for sea-run trout in the tidal zone during October to December is popular.

WAIRAU RIVER AND ITS TRIBUTARIES

Rising in the Raglan and Spenser ranges, this large, sometimes blue-coloured river flows north to Blenheim. The upper reaches are stable, swift and single-channelled, until emerging into the main valley where the riverbed can be 1 km wide. Here it is braided with many side channels and islands. From Renwick to the sea it is once again confined to a single channel. Fishing for resident and sea-run brown trout is surprisingly productive. Good spotting conditions are common once the snow is gone. Trout up to 3 kg – and some trophies – are often caught, with all methods being successful.

HANG YOUR HOOK

Wairepo House
Weka Road
Matiri
RD2 Upper Moutere
Nelson
03 526 6865
wairepo@xtra.co.nz
designed to capture sea and mountain views

Mi Casa
Hunters Moon
Rowling Heights Road
Kaiteriteri
RD2 Motueka
03 527 8073
self-contained annex to home on Kaiteriteri Bay

Golden Bay Lodge
State Highway 60
Tukurua
RD2 Takaka
Goldenbaylodge@xtra.co.nz
www.GoldenBayLodge@co.nz
on a cliff-top overlooking Golden Bay

Kahurangi Luxury Retreat
State Highway 60
Takaka
RD2 Golden Bay
Kahurangi@xtra.co.nz
www.webnz.com/kahurangi
luxury retreat close to Kahurangi and Abel Tasman National Parks

CATCH A MEAL

Herzog Luxury Restaurant and Winery
81 Jeffries Road
Blenheim
03 572 8770
info@herzog.co.nz
www.herzog.co.nz
Mediterranean cuisine and fine cellar wines

The Mussel Boys Restaurant
73 Main Road
Havelock
03 574 2824
musselboys@xtra.co.nz
www.musselboys.co.nz
seafood specialists

Akbabas Turkish Kebab House
130 Bridge Street
Nelson
03 545 8825
akbaba@ts.co.nz
Middle Eastern cuisine

Waimea Estates
22 Appleby Highway
Hope
03 544 4963
waimeaestates@ts.co.nz
www.waimeaestates.co.nz
Nelson food and wine

Appleman's
294 Queen Street
Richmond
03 544 0610
seafood a speciality

Bencarri Farm Café
McCallums Road
Takaka
03 525 8261
bencarri@voyager.co.nz
www.bencarrifarm.co.nz
beside the Anatoki River

Boatshed Café and Restaurant
350 Wakefield Quay
Nelson
03 546 9783
the.boatshed@xtra.co.nz
specialises in seafood

Broccoli Row Café
5 Buxton Square
Nelson
03 548 9621
seafood and vegetarian

Mapua Naturesmoke
Mapua Wharf
Mapua
03 540 2280
tomfox@iconz.co.nz
smoked seafood

The Grape Escape Café and Wine Bar
McShane Road
Richmond
03 544 4341
lara.allan@xtra.co.nz
local cuisine and wines

WHEN THE FISH DON'T BITE

Abel Tasman Seal Swim
Valley Road
Marahau
Motueka
03 527 8136
sealswim@ihug.co.nz
www.sealswim.co.nz
swim with the seals in Abel Tasman National Park

Dolphin Watch Marlborough
PO Box 197
Picton
03 573 8040
dolphin.Marlborough@xtra.co.nz
www.dolphinwatchmarlborough.co.nz
seals and dolphins in Queen Charlotte Sound

The Sounds Connection
10 London Quay
Picton
03 573 8843
sounds.connection@xtra.co.nz
www.soundsconnection.co.nz
small group fishing charters in Queen Charlotte Sound

Abel Tasman National Park Experiences
265 High Street
Motueka
03 528 7675
ate@abeltasman.co.nz
www.abeltasman.co.nz
one-day sea kayaking trips available

Stonehurst Farm Horse Treks
Stonehurst Farm
Clover Road
Richmond
03 542 4121
suzanne@stonehurstfarm.co.nz
www.stonehurstfarm.co.nz
treks from one to four hours

Airborn Paragliding
George Harvey Road
Upper Moutere
03 548 5520
maco@paradise.net.nz
tandem paragliding

Wine Tours by Bike
56 George Street
Blenheim
03 577 6954
ryan@winetoursbybike.co.nz
www.winetoursbybike.co.nz
not far to fall after wine tasting

Farewell Spit Safari
Tasman Street
Collingwood
03 524 8257
enquiries@farewellspit.co.nz
www.FarewellSpit.co.nz
eco-tours on the world's longest sand spit

Highlight Tours
15A Murphy's Road
Blenheim
03 577 9046
Highlight.tours@xtra.co.nz
www.marlborough.co.nz/highlight/
half-day tours of Marlborough

Buller Experience – Jetboat Tours
PO Box 42
Murchison
03 523 9880
pete@murchison.co.nz
www.murchison.co.nz
jetboat the mighty Buller River

Ultimate Descents
51 Fairfax Street
Murchison
03 523 9899
ultimate@rivers.co.nz
www.rivers.co.nz
raft the Buller and Karamea Rivers

North Canterbury

North Canterbury is almost the antithesis of its diverse neighbouring Fish and Game New Zealand region to the north. The Canterbury region has but two main topographical features – high country on the foothills and eastern slopes of the Southern Alps, and a broad and mostly featureless plain leading to the Pacific coast. So the fishing waters tend to come in just two types as well – there are high-country streams and the snowmelt-fed headwaters of rivers, and there are wide and braided shingle rivers stretching across the plains.

It is the prolific runs of spawning salmon entering these large, braided rivers – such as the Rakaia and Waimakariri – that give the North Canterbury region its reputation as a salmon fishery. Trout fishing runs a distant second. Yet for all that, the dual-feature region does offer trout-fishing opportunities that are not to be scoffed at. The braided rivers may not be prime trout habitat but they do hold sea-run brown trout that tend to get taken by salmon fishermen using spin fishing tackle. These sea-run browns can be large and numerous at times during the season. The best fishing time is often in the evening after a hot day when the browns follow prey species from the sea into the mouth and lagoon areas to feed.

Many streams on the Canterbury Plains become too low and clear during summer months to provide good fishing, and so it pays to get in early during the first few months of the season. On the other hand, the mountain rivers and streams provide an excellent back-country trout fishery – but one that is generally neither for the faint of limb nor for the cast-and-hope brigade. Prime brown trout in these clear waters need to be stalked and fished with skill and patience. The middle of the day when the sun is highest is the best time as the fish are

FAMOUS FOR
• Whale-watching at Kaikoura
• The Crusaders rugby team
• Mt Hutt ski area
• Canterbury lamb
• The Christchurch Wizard
• Christchurch Cathedral
• Standardbred horses
• Colourful gardens

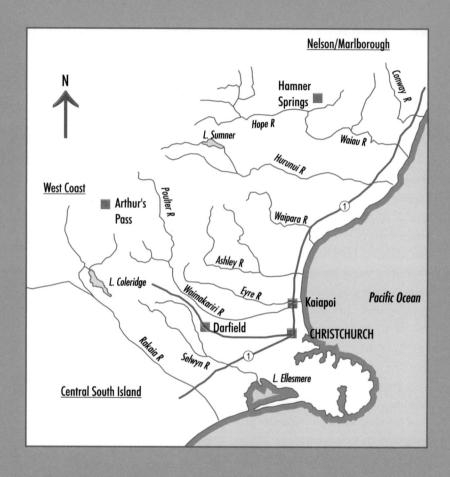

more easily spotted. Fishing tends to demand a lot of walking, but once the fish are located they can be quite easy to catch compared to high-country trout in other regions. Fly fishing is the most common method for high-country river fishing but spin fishing is also effective.

The Waimakariri River is a nationally important wildlife habitat, ranging from the pristine-based alpine streams in the mountain areas of the Southern Alps, to estuarine areas in its lower reaches. The river supports 29 different animal species, and Chinook salmon, brown and rainbow trout are the main sports fish species found in the river. Because of its recreational importance, the Waimakariri is carefully monitored to ensure that agriculture and irrigation does not ruin its water quality and adversely affect the wildlife habitat.

Fishing aside, the North Canterbury region is one of New Zealand's most popular tourist destinations. The opportunities for adventure range from whale-watching at Kaikoura to skiing in the Southern Alps – and Christchurch is urbane New Zealand at its best.

INFORMATION

Fish and Game New Zealand North Canterbury region
3 Horatio Street
Christchurch
03 366 9191
fishandgame@clear.net.nz
www.fishandgame.org.nz
Regional manager: Ross Millichamp
Administration manager: Brian Webb
Field officers: Brian Ross, Steve Terry
Environment officer: Rochelle Hardy

Canterbury Anglers' Club
The Secretary
PO Box 1602
Christchurch

Canterbury Flyfishing Club
G. Caldwell
PO Box 13591
Christchurch

Christchurch Visitor Information Centre
Cathedral Square
Christchurch
03 379 9629
info@christchurchnz.net
www.christchurchnz.net

Hurunui Visitor Information Centre
Main Road
Hanmer
03 315 7128
info@hurunui.govt.nz
www.hurunui@govt.nz

Christchurch Fishing and Casting Club
Fay Mangos
6 Haslett Place
Riccarton
Christchurch
03 942 8226

WHERE AND WHAT

Fish and Game New Zealand's North Canterbury region is divided into two zones – eastern and western – which corresponds with high-country streams and river headwaters in the foothills of the Southen Alps, and the lowland Canterbury Plains area where the rivers become wide and braided. Fishing regulations tend to be more restrictive in high-country waters.

The eastern zone is to the east of a line extending from the Rakaia River, near the Coleridge Power Station, to Woodstock on the Waimakariri River, to the Oxford–Glentui Road bridge on the Ashley River, to the junction of the Hurunui River with the South Branch, to the junction of the Waiau and Hope Rivers; and excluding Lake Rubicon. The western zone is the area to the west of the eastern zone plus Lake Rubicon.

The region has more than 30 high-country lakes holding brown and rainbow trout as well as landlocked salmon. The high-country rivers have small fish numbers and the fishing – usually fly fishing to sighted fish – is challenging. Trout populations are greater on small low-country rivers and streams, although fish size is usually small to medium. Access to some small low-country rivers is over private property and landowner permission is required. Sea-run brown trout provide exciting summer fishing in the lower reaches of the larger low-country rivers. At times during the season the browns are big and plentiful.

The North Canterbury regulations follow the general South Island regulations. Waters open to fishing all year round are the eastern zone reaches of the Rakaia, Waimakariri, Ashley, Hurunui, and Waiau rivers; the Avon and Heathcote rivers; Selwyn River – from the Upper Selwyn Huts to Lake Ellesmere; the downstream sections of the Cam; the South Branch of the Waimakariri, Styx, Wairewa, Kaiapoi, Okuti and Halswell Rivers; the lower sections of the Halswell canal; Monopolies Pond; and Lakes Rotokohatu, Forsyth, and Kaiapoi.

The upper Kaiapoi River is open from 1 October to 28 February and all other rivers and lakes in the eastern zone are open from 1 October to 30 April. On Broken River and its tributaries the trout-fishing season opens on 3 November and closes on 30 April. The open season for trout fishing on the Rakaia River and tributaries in the western zone is from 1 October to 31 March; and on the Wilberforce Diversion (including the Wilberforce Canal and Oakden Canal) and all rivers flowing into western zone lakes, from 1 December to 31 March. The trout season for all other rivers in the western zone is 1 October to 30 April and for lakes from 3 November to 30 April. There is a winter season from 1 June to 31 August on Lake Coleridge and from 1 June to 30 September on Lakes Selfe, Lyndon, Pearson,Taylor and Sumner, and Loch Katrine.

The Kaiapoi Lakes, Ashley River above the Oxford–Glentui Road bridge, and Broken River and all of its tributaries are catch-and-release fisheries. There is generally a daily bag limit of two trout throughout the region, except on Lake Coleridge and Lake Sumner where the limit is four.

Casting around

A comprehensive fishing guide, *Fishing Access: A Guide to Popular Fishing Locations in the North Canterbury Fish & Game Region*, is available free from tackle shops and the regional Fish and Game office.

THE RAKAIA RIVER

The Rakaia is a large, snowfed, braided river which supports good runs of sea-run trout in the lower reaches. November through to the end of February are the prime months. Trout are also present in the headwaters, although the river is best known as a salmon fishery.

The Mouth to SH1

Access to this part of the river, where sea-run browns are caught among the salmon, is best on the south side. All access roads run off Acton Rd.

Above SH1

A number of good access roads lead off Rakaia Terrace Road, including the Gun Club, Darrochs Road, Steeles Road and Sleemans Road. Fishing is best in summer's low-water conditions, and local knowledge is almost essential.

Above The Rakaia Gorge

A road leads up the south side of the river from which access is good. Take the turn-off to Glenfalloch, a few kilometres on the south side of the gorge bridge. This road meets the river about 10 km above the gorge. The fishing is difficult and patchy.

TACKLE BOX

The Complete Angler
cnr Cashel & Barbadoes Streets
Christchurch
03 366 9885

Mikes Fishing
27 Armagh Street
Christchurch
03 365 7146

Fishermans Loft
72 Riccarton Road
Christchurch
03 348 8836

Angler Accessories
42 Maces Road
Bromley
Christchurch
03 384 1477

There are also two good trout-fishing streams in the upper Rakaia catchment – the Glenariffe Stream and the Hydra Waters, but the trout are easily spooked.

THE WAIMAKARIRI RIVER

This river is similar in many respects to the Rakaia, however, because it is close to Christchurch it tends to get congested during salmon runs. The Waimakariri is the most heavily used recreational river in the South Island. It has good runs of sea-run brown trout and access is excellent.

McIntosh's Rocks

A popular fishing spot about 2 km from the mouth that is reached from Ferry Road, which veers off the Kaiapoi–Kairaki Road. Although best known for salmon fishing, McIntosh's can also provide good trout fishing, especially around dawn and dusk.

GUIDES AND CHARTERS

Kevin Frazier
104 Elizabeth Street
Ashburton
03 308 5963

Shane Johnston
20 Powell Crescent
Avonhead
Christchurch
03 358 6223

Chappie Chapman
31 Charlcott Street
Russley
Christchurch
03 359 5440
chapp@xtra.co.nz
www.chappie.co.nz

Tony Allan
65 Ocean View Tce
Christchurch
03 326 5611
angler@xtra.co.nz

Nigel Birt
32 Settlers Cres
Ferrymead
Christchurch
03 384 8945
www.backcountry.co.nz

Bill Allison
211 West Belt
Rangiora
03 313 8007

Basil Ivey
Cairn Hollow
RD5 Ashburton
03 303 6078

Steve Gerard
13 Cameron Street
Methven
03 302 8448
Steve.Gerard@xtra.co.nz
www.flyfishing.co.nz

Mark Eastmond
157 Lower Flat Road
Waiau
North Canterbury
03 315 6173

Lower and middle reaches

A system of riverside roads and stopbanks on both sides of the river give good access to the Waimakariri, although the trout fishing is fairly indifferent. The river is severely affected by wind and it is generally more suited to spin fishing. At the Waimakariri Gorge bridge on SH73 anglers can reach both sides of the river. The most popular is on the south side of the bridge where a shingle track leads down the terrace and out onto the riverbed. The gorge holds some large browns.

Above the Gorge

The best fishing is in the upper reaches, which you can get to wherever SH73 gets close to or crosses the river. This stretch starts just past the Cass township and runs until the Bealey Bridge. Access to the north side is off a shingle track just before SH73 reaches the Waimakariri. This track leads down the terrace to the Mt White Bridge.

THE HURUNUI RIVER

The Hurunui is a reliably good brown trout fishery.

The mouth

Sea-run trout are found around the river mouth in the early part of the season. The north side of the mouth is the easiest to reach. Take the first road to the right while heading north out of the small town of Domett on SH1. A well-defined track at the road end leads down a steep hill to the north side of the mouth. The south

CATCH A MEAL

The Craypot Café and Bar
70 West End
Kaikoura
03 319 6027
crayfish and seafood

Nor' Wester Café and Bar
95 Main North Road
Amberley
03 314 9411
cultured dining oasis

Pescatore Seafood Restaurant
The George
50 Park Tce
Christchurch
03 371 0257
stunning seafood in a magical setting

Hays
63 Victoria Street
Christchurch
03 379 7501
eat@foodandwine.co.nz
www.foodandwine.co.nz
Canterbury lamb is the speciality

Pegasus Arms
Oxford Tce
Christchurch
03 366 0600
Christchurch's oldest remaining residential building

125

side of the mouth is reached from the road to Napenape.

Middle reaches

The reaches above the mouth are easily accessed where SH1 crosses the river – a track leads off the road on the north side of the bridge. The river can also be accessed from SH7 on both sides of the Balmoral bridge. On the south side a track leads off the main road on the downstream side and out to the river. Access on the north side is had by taking the first right-hand turn past the bridge, and turning back toward the river (signposted) a few hundred metres up the road.

Upper reaches

The upper reaches of the Hurunui provide good back-country fishing for anglers prepared to do some walking. Access is from the Lake Sumner Road, which mostly runs alongside the river until it reaches the Sister's Stream. The river splits into a north and south branch partway up this road. The north branch is fed from Lake Sumner and tends to be more stable and clear most of the time. A 10 km stretch holds high stocks of brown trout up to 3.5 kg in deep pools and swift runs. There are also some rainbows. There are fewer fish in the headwaters of the south branch, which is subject to frequent flooding.

CATCH A MEAL

Palazzo del Marinaio
108 Hereford Street
The Shades Arcade
Christchurch
03 365 4640
montebello@xtra.co.nz
www.palazzo.co.nz
seafood the Italian way

China Town Restaurant
The Mall
Methven
03 302 8882
Asian à la carte

Sweethearts Restaurant
Berryfields Berryfruit Farm
161 Gardiners Road
Christchurch
03 359 5630
bruntonandrea@hotmail.com
www.sweethearts.co.nz
award-winning country restaurant surrounded by fields of berries

The Lodge on Chertsey
Mt Hutt Village
Methven
03 303 2000
thelodgenz@xtra.co.nz
Methven's newest upmarket lodge

HANG YOUR HOOK

Albergo Hanmer
88 Rippingale Road
Hanmer Springs
03 315 7428
albergohanmer@hotmail.com
www.albergohanmer.com
majestic mountain views and gourmet breakfast

Braemar Lodge
283 Medway Road
Hanmer Springs
03 315 7049
relax@braemarlodge.co.nz
www.braemarlodge.co.nz
panoramic views of the Southen Alps

The Old Convent
cnr Mill and Mount Fyffe Roads
Kaikoura
03 319 6603
o.convent@xtra.co.nz
superb French cuisine

Sherwood Lodge
Sherwood Road
Waiau
North Canterbury
03 315 6078
comfort on a high-country sheep station

The Old Glenmark Vicarage
161 Church Road
Waipara
North Canterbury
03 314 6775
restored kauri villa

Okuku Country Lodge
Rakahuri Road
Rangiora
RD4 North Canterbury
03 312 8740
okuku@ihug.co.nz
sumptuous meals and an indoor heated swimming pool

Tyrone Deer Farm
RD12 Rakaia
Mid Canterbury
03 302 8096
guides available from this countrystay B&B

Waituna
Waikari
North Canterbury
03 314 4575
waitunawaikari@hotmail.com
rambling homestead halfway between Hanmer Springs and Christchurch

The Charlotte Jane
110 Papanui Road
Merivale
Christchurch
03 355 1028
charjane@ihug.co.nz
cosy restored villa with fine dining adjacent

Sportsman's Lodge
6 Ennerdale Row
Westmorland
Christchurch
03 339 8633
nzhunt@xtra.co.nz
www.nzhuntingandfishing.com
guided trips to back-country waters

Gunyah Country Lodge
Sleemans Road
Glenroy
Canterbury
03 318 6504
relax@gunyah.co.nz
salmon and trout fishing close at hand

Grasmere Lodge
State Highway 73
near Cass
03 318 8407
retreat@grasmere.co.nz
www.grasmere.co.nz
luxury in a splendid mountain setting

THE WAIAU RIVER

The Waiau is the most northern of the major rivers in the North Canterbury region and gets the least fishing pressure. The best trout fishing is in the upper reaches where fish up to 4.5 kg can be found in its clear pools. The headwaters run through the old Ada Station on the St James Walkway and landowner permission is needed to get into the upper Waiau. Most of the gin-clear headwater streams hold sizeable browns.

There is good access to the river's middle reaches at the Waiau township, Leslie Hills and Hanmer Ferry Bridges. Above Hanmer, anywhere the road comes next to the river is a good starting point.

NORTH CANTERBURY LAKES

Lake Coleridge

Lake Coleridge is the largest and most heavily fished lake in North Canterbury. It supports one of the very few New Zealand populations of landlocked Chinook salmon. Brown and rainbow trout are also abundant, although rainbow trout tend to be more 'catchable'. Opening Weekend (the first Saturday in November) is a big event with hundreds of anglers on the lake and lots of fish being caught. There are many popular fishing areas around the lake.

Lake Lyndon

Lake Lyndon, reached off SH73 near Porters Pass, yields good catches of rainbow and brown trout. Fish numbers have dropped but the fish are larger.

Lake Pearson

Pearson is one of the larger North Canterbury lakes. Mackinaw (American lake trout) are present in the lake but are seldom caught. Those that are caught tend to come from the eastern end of the lake. Brown trout are the most common catch. Lake Pearson is easily accessed from SH73, which runs along the southern shore.

WHEN THE FISH DON'T BITE

Whale Watch Kaikoura
0800 655 121
03 319 6767
res@whalewatch.co.nz
www.whalewatch.co.nz
giant sperm whales up close

Dust 'n' Dirt mountain biking
20 Conical Hill Road
Hanmer Springs
03 315 7233
head downhill on a mountain bike

International Antarctic Centre
Christchurch International Airport
0508 736 4846
www.iceberg.co.nz
emperor penguins on ice

Punting in the Park
Antigua Boat Sheds
2 Cambridge Tce
03 366 0337
take a punt through the Botanic Gardens

Mt Cook Salmon
Canal Road
Mackenzie District
03 435 0085
the next best thing to trout

Jet Thrills
Merivale
Christchurch
0800 847 455
jet-boat thrills

Alpine Horse Safaris
Waitohi Downs
Hawarden
North Canterbury
03 314 4293
alpinehorse@xtra.co.nz
www.alpinehorse.co.nz
ride over high mountain passes

Waimak River Horse Treks
129 Coutts Island Road
Belfast
Christchurch
03 356 1145
mcstay@ihug.co.nz
horse riding close to Christchurch

High Country Explorer
PO Box 1610
Christchurch
0800 863 975
high-country@xtra.co.nz
drive 20 km across 35,000 acre Flock Hill sheep station by 4WD

TranzAlpine (The)
TranzRail
Christchurch Railway Station
Christchurch
0800 802 802
passengerservices@tranzrail.co.nz
www.tranzrailtravel.co.nz
cross the Canterbury Plains and the Southern Alps to Greymouth by train

TranzCoastal Pacific (The)
TranzRail
Christchurch Railway Station
Christchurch
0800 802 802
passengerservices@tranzrail.co.nz
www.tranzrailtravel.co.nz
follow the coast to Kaikoura

Wilson's Mill Garden
3 Christmas Road
Ohoka
Christchurch
03 327 8113
wilsonsmill@xtra.co.nz
a 16 acre garden brimming with plants of many varieties, including roses and perennials

LOW-COUNTRY RIVERS

The Selwyn River

The Selwyn contains reasonable numbers of brown trout in the lower reaches but is often dry and flows underground in the middle reaches. Most fishing is in the stretch from the Upper Selwyn Huts to the mouth, where access is good. Fly fishing is best after dark.

Harts Creek

Harts Creek is a good fly fishing stream, especially towards the mouth. Follow Lake Road to its intersection with Timber Yard Road (heading south), turn left down the latter and turn left again onto a small bridge not far from the corner. A car-parking area is at the end of the track and a DoC walkway leads down to the mouth. Fishing at the mouth is good after dark, but the river between the car park and the mouth offers good fly fishing during daylight hours. Access to the river above the car park requires the consent of the landowner.

South Branch of the Waimakariri

The South Branch contains good populations of smaller fish and is a very popular 'after work' fishery. The river is reached at the Dickies Road bridge or through the Groynes picnic area. From the Groynes you can fish either upstream or downstream of the main picnic areas.

West Coast

Unique is a word that it is usually best to avoid. But if there is one region in New Zealand that can be labelled unique without fear of challenge and embarrassment, it is the West Coast of the South Island.

The coast is a long, narrow ribbon of just a few kilometres between the Tasman Sea and the soaring, snowcapped peaks of the Southern Alps. Situated on an alpine fault, it is an area constantly being thrust into the sky by crashing tectonic plates – and just as quickly being washed down to size by ferocious weather blowing in from Australia and the Southern Ocean. The soil – in geological terms, just recently pushed out of the sea – is poor, yet on it grow towering rainforests. The land is rich in other ways too. Maori mined the rivers for pounamu (greenstone), which New Zealand's tangata whenua used in place of metal, and Europeans rushed to the Coast in the 1860s infected with gold-fever.

Yet for all its special geography and geology, glaciers, national parks and a World Heritage area, it is the people of the West Coast that are perhaps the most distinctive feature of the region. Coasters are legendary – tough, independent, resourceful and parochial. They are also extraordinarily friendly, extending a hospitality rarely matched elsewhere in the country. You could say that trout fishing on the coast is a bit like the people who live there – it is not a pursuit for the fainthearted.

FAMOUS FOR

- Franz Josef and Fox Glaciers
- White heron colony at Okarito
- Punakaiki Pancake Rocks
- After-hours drinking
- Seal colonies
- Kumara, start of the Coast to Coast multisport event
- World Heritage Area forests
- Whitebait
- Wild Foods Festival
- Gold-mining
- Greenstone deposits
- Coal

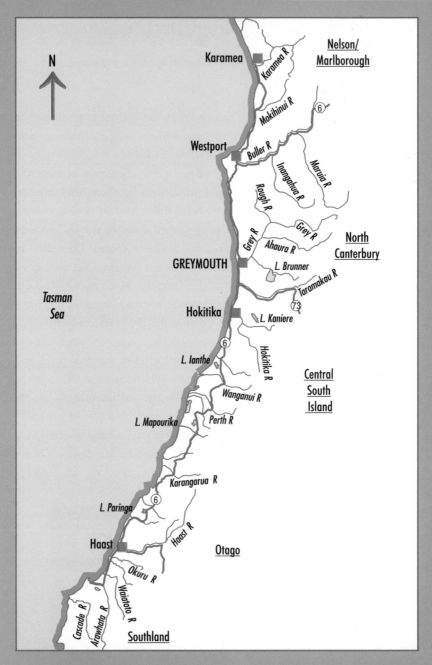

N

Nelson/
Marlborough

Karamea

Karamea R

Mokihinui R

⑥

Westport

Buller R

Inangahua R

Maruia R

Rough R

Grey R

Grey R

North
Canterbury

Ahaura R

GREYMOUTH

L. Brunner

Taramakau R

⑦⑶

Hokitika

L. Kaniere

Tasman
Sea

Hokitika R

L. Ianthe

⑥

Central
South
Island

Wanganui R

L. Mapourika

Perth R

Karangarua R

L. Paringa

⑥

Haast

Haast R

Otago

Okuru R

Waiatoto R

Cascade R

Arawhata R

Southland

The distance between mountains and sea is short and steep and so are the rivers. Yet they carry the spoils of an astonishing rainfall – more than 6 m deep in places – and flow through some of the most rugged country and dense bush in New Zealand; places where few people, if any, have been. It is wild and spectacularly scenic. Yet these primeval rivers hold trout, good trout. In fact, those prepared to make the effort to explore the wilderness consider that the West Coast offers the best fly fishing for brown trout in New Zealand – and peace, solitude and a superb environment are guaranteed.

The fishing is not all hard, however. There are some lakes that fish particularly well, and closer to the sea the rivers slow and become easier to access and to fish; many attract sea-run brown trout. Aside from fishing, there is no shortage of things to do on the Coast, although most involve other outdoor pursuits. If that doesn't suit, there is no better place in which to just stand and stare in awe at the beauty of nature.

INFORMATION

Fish and Game New Zealand West Coast region
Airport Drive
Hokitika
03 755 8546
fish&game@minidata.co.nz
www.fishandgame.org.nz
Manager: Chris Tonkin
Field Officer: Ian Hadland

Westport Visitor Information Centre
1 Brougham Street
Westport
03 789 6658
Westport.info@xtra.co.nz
www.westport.org.nz

Greymouth Visitor Information Centre
cnr Mackay and Herbert Streets
Greymouth
03 768 5101
vingm@minidata.co.nz
www.westcoastbookings.co.nz

Westland Visitor Information Centre
cnr Hamilton and Tancred Streets
Hokitika
03 755 6166
hkkvin@xtra.co.nz
www.westlanddc.govt.nz

Hokitika Angling Club
PO Box 174
Hokitika
Contact: Des Johnston
03 755 6724

Grey District Angling Club
K. Dalzell
4 Wilson Cresent
Greymouth
03 768 5739

Dayaram Ganda
03 768 9910
dganda@xtra.co

WHERE AND WHAT

Fish and Game New Zealand's West Coast region runs for 800 km along the South Island's west coast from Kahurangi Point, north of Karamea, to Awarua Point south of Haast, and to seaward of the Southern Alps mountain chain. In between lies 2 million ha of land, much of it wilderness and containing a huge diversity of challenging angling opportunities.

Brown trout on the West Coast are found from headwater streams to tidal river mouths. Scenic lakes and springfed streams are also a feature of the region. Trout numbers in the rivers fluctuate depending on the time of year.

The usual pattern is for the lower reaches to carry more fish in spring and early summer, after which trout move upstream to occupy mid-headwater habitats. Smaller streams generally fish best in early season before water temperatures increase and trout become active for shorter periods. There is good access to most fishing waters with only the Coast's capricious climate and rugged terrain putting up any sort of barrier.

The West Coast region's fishing regulations follow the general South Island freshwater fishing regulations. Many of the region's lakes and the lower reaches of rivers and streams are open for fishing all year round but reaches above SH6 and SH67 and the headwaters are closed between 30 April and 1 October.

The waters open all year round are the Big Wanganui, Cascade, Arnold, Hapuka, Kaniere, Okarito, and Whataroa Rivers; downstream reaches of the Jacobs, Arahura, Arawhata, Big Totara, Buller, Cook, Grey, Haast, Hokitika, Karamea, Karangarua, Kohaihai, Kokatahi, Little Totara, Little Wanganui, Mahitahi, Mikonui, Moeraki, Mokihinui, New, Ngakawau, Nile, Okari, Okuru, Omoeroa, Oparara, Orawaiti, Paringa, Poerua, Porarari, Punakaiki, Taramakau, Totara, Turnbull, Waiatoto, Waikukupa, Waimangaroa, Waita, Waitaha, Whakapohi and Whareatea Rivers; and Lakes Ianthe, Brunner, Moeraki, Mapourika, Ellery, Paringa, Mahinapua, Wahapo and Kaniere. The closed season applies to other waters.

There is a daily bag limit of two trout on the Murray, Harris, Duck, Larrys, Molloy, Deep, and Stony Creeks; and the Ohikanui, Waitahu, Rough, Haupiri, Crooked, Orangipuku, Big, and Moonlight Rivers; the upper reaches of the Karamea and Mokinui Rivers, and the Bruce Stream. On other waters the daily limit is four, of which no more than two may be rainbow trout.

There is no length restriction on trout in the region except on Lakes Mapourika, Paringa, Moeraki and Ellery where the minimum length is 25 cm.

Casting around

LAKES

Lake Brunner

Lake Brunner, 25 km from Greymouth on the Arnold Valley Road, holds brown trout averaging 1.1 kg and is the most popular angling water in the region. The lake can be reached on foot over the Arnold river footbridge at Moana village. Other parts of the lakeshore can be reached by driving past Moana to Iveagh Bay and Mitchells. Trolling near the lake outlet during summer is popular, and fly fishing from shore at the lake outlet during early morning or late evening or at the mouth of Crooked and Hohonu Rivers during the day for cruising fish works well. Fly fishing from boat over the shallow weed beds between Orangipuku and Te Kinga is also productive.

Lake Poerua

Lake Poerua is a 24 km drive from Moana and holds well-conditioned brown trout averaging 1.8 kg. Trolling and harling is successful over most of the lake. Fly fishing is productive but is easiest from a boat. The narrow neck halfway up the lake and around shallow margins are the most popular locations.

Lake Haupiri

Haupiri, 42 km from Greymouth on SH7, also holds medium-sized browns. The lake is difficult to reach on foot and a boat is almost essential. Fly fishing off the mouths of the small feeder streams on the southern side of the lake offers the best chance of success.

GUIDES AND CHARTERS

John Boyles
RD1 Blackball
Greymouth
03 732 3531
John@iky.net.nz

David Heine
111 Shakespeare Street
Greymouth
03 768 6415

Silvio Edmund
9 Larsen Street
Cape Foulwind
RD2 Westport
03 789 5686
s.s.s.@xtra.co.nz

Gavin Pegley
RD2 Blue Spur
Hokitika
03 755 6874
tightlines@xtra.co.nz

135

Lake Mapourika

Mapourika is adjacent to SH6, 10 km north of Franz Josef and is a productive brown trout fishery. In calm conditions large brown trout are easily spotted cruising lake margins and respond to a bully imitation if fly fishing or small dark lure when spin fishing. Best spots are along the western fringe south of the lake outlet, off the entrance to Jetty Bay, or off the roadside edge from Jetty Bay to the mouth of Redjacks Creek.

Lake Paringa

This lake next to SH6 south of Fox Glacier is well stocked with 1–2 kg brown trout. The shallow margins near the lake outlet suit harling or fishing with light lures.

TACKLE BOX

Hokitika Cycles & Sportsworld
33 Tancred Street
Hokitika
03 755 8662

Greymouth Sports
123 Mackay Street
Greymouth
03 768 6175

Aim West Sports
20 Weld Street
Hokitika
03 755 8481

Reefton Sports Centre
56 Broadway
Reefton
03 732 8593

West Coast Fishing and Firearms
10 Tainui Street
Greymouth
03 768 0206

Lake Mahinapua

Turn off SH6 at Mahinapua Hotel 12 km south of Hokitika. The lake holds some trout but you are more likely to hook one of the lake's large perch population and a boat is necessary.

Lake Moeraki

A boat is almost a necessity on this scenic gem between Paringa and Haast on SH6, although cruising fish can often be seen from the road near the western margin. For fly fishers a bully imitation is the staple lure, but trout will rise to terrestrial imitations.

Lake Ianthe

Lake Ianthe is south of Ross on SH6 near Pukekura and is an excellent brown trout fishery. This lake produces beautifully marked fish up to 2.5 kg. Prolific weed beds make deep trolling difficult near the edges, but harling with a feathered lure can be successful. Casting a bully imitation fly or a nymph to cruising fish under the bush-fringed margin are good methods in suitable conditions. Watch also for subtle rises near the weed beds.

RIVERS NORTH OF GREYMOUTH

Karamea River

The lower reaches of the Karamea River up to the gorge can be reached by crossing farmland on either side of the river; seek permission and leave gates as you find them. While trout may be spotted feeding in the early morning, the lower reaches are mostly fished 'blind'. The Karamea Gorge walking route leads to the wild upper reaches.

Little Wanganui River

This river has good fishing from the Wangapeka Valley or Blue Duck (south bank) but landowner permission is needed for access. The upper reaches are wild and scenic requiring a minor expedition or helicopter to reach. Spin fishing is best in the larger holes and runs in middle and lower section although in normal flows fish can be spotted feeding in the early morning and evening. In midsummer 'blind' dry fly fishing can also be rewarding.

Arnold River

The Arnold, which drains Lake Brunner, joins the Grey River 15 km from Greymouth at Stillwater. It holds high numbers of medium-sized brown trout and is fishable in all but extreme weather conditions. There are several marked access points along the Arnold Valley Road. The Arnold is popular with fly anglers especially during the prolific evening hatches of October/ November and March/April. Fly fishing is the most successful method.

Lower Grey River

The lower Grey River catch-rate is amongst the highest in the region. There are numerous medium-sized brown trout for the taking in the lower river and larger trout in the tributaries, which are fisheries in their own right.

HANG YOUR HOOK

River View Lodge
State Highway 6
Buller Gorge Road
Westport
03 789 6037
riverview@voyager.co.nz
overlooking the Buller River, 7 km from Westport

Lake Brunner Lodge
Mitchells
Lake Brunner
Westland
03 738 0163
lodge@brunner.co.nz
one of New Zealand's most renowned fishing lodges

The Rocks Homestay
Hartmount Place
PO Box 16
Punakaiki
03 731 1141
therocks@minidata.co.nz
close to the famous blowholes and rocks

Kapitea Ridge Country Lodge
Chesterfield Road
Kapitea Creek
RD2 Hokitika
03 755 6805
kapitea@minidata.co.nz
www.kapitea.co.nz
modern lodge overlooking the coast

Villa Polenza
Brickfield Road
RD2 Hokitika
03 755 7801
villapolenza@xtra.co.nz
Italian-style villa overlooking Hokitika with panoramic views of the Southern Alps

Craidenlie Lodge
Blue Spur
PO Box 182
Hokitika
03 755 5063
bruce@craidenlielodge.co.nz
www.craidenlielodge.co.nz
a fourth generation Coaster will share his love of the region with you

Waiho Stables Country Stay
Docherty Creek
Franz Josef Glacier
West Coast
03 752 0747
waiho@minidata.co.nz
the backdrop doesn't get any better

Wapiti Park Homestead
State Highway 6
Harihari
03 753 3074
wapitipark@minidata.co.nz
rural accommodation near the renowned brown trout fishery, La Fontaine Stream

Carrickfergus
Roberston Road
Harihari
03 753 3124
carrickfergus@actrix.co.nz
pit your skills against brown trout in local springfed streams

Matai Lodge
Whataroa
South Westland
03 753 4156
jpurcell@xtra.co.nz
'a stranger is a friend we have yet to meet'

There is excellent access with roading on both sides of the river up to Ikamatua. Where the river does not run alongside the road, permission must be obtained from landowners to cross their land. Fly fishing is best in the evening when fish often rise to hatches of flies at dusk, although fishing with heavy nymphs can be productive during the day, particularly in shallow riffles.

Upper Ahaura and Haupiri Rivers

The Haupiri and Ahaura Rivers, reached via the Greymouth to Reefton highway, both contain good numbers of medium to large trout although numbers are fewer in the upper reaches. The best fishing in the Ahaura River is from the Nancy River confluence downstream. In the Haupiri River fish density is highest in the first few kilometres downstream of the lake outlet. Access to the upper Haupiri, which usually holds good fish numbers, requires landowner permission. The upper Ahaura, which consistently produces a few good-sized fish, is rough and difficult to get to and anglers need to be fit.

Mawheraiti (Little Grey) River

This is a tributary of the Grey River joining at Ikamatua (between Greymouth and Reefton). The Mawheraiti River is a gently flowing tea-coloured stream usually holding high numbers of small to medium trout. It is reached from the Atarau Road bridge or from both bridges where SH7 crosses the Mawheraiti River. Fly fishing works well and spin fishing is effective during freshes, particularly in lower reaches.

Rough River

The Rough also enters the Grey River at Ikamatua and provides challenging fishing for predominantly large brown trout. The lower reaches are accessed from the Atarau Road bridge and the upper reaches via Mirfins Road. Water clarity is usually high and best suits dry fly and nymph techniques for fish that become more wary as the season progresses.

Ohikanui River

The Ohikanui, 32 km east of Westport along SH6, is full of large boulders

CATCH A MEAL

Ashley Hotel
74 Tasman Street
Greymouth
03 768 5135
ashley.grey@xtra.co.nz
specialising in West Coast delicacies

Bay House Café
Beach Road
Tauranga Bay
Westport
03 789 7133
bayhouse@xtra.co.nz
dine@bayhousecafe.co.nz
www.bayhousecafe.co.nz
voted best café three years in a row

Southland Hotel
111 Revell Street
Hokitika
03 755 8344
elegant hotel restaurant in tranquil setting

Café de Paris
19–21 Tancred Street
Hokitika
03 755 8933
award-winning Provençal cuisine

Beeches Restaurant
Franz Josef
Franz Josef Glacier
03 752 0721
Beeches@xtra.co.nz
relaxed atmosphere in natural surroundings

Punakaiki Rocks Hotel
State Highway 6
Punakaiki
Barrytown
03 731 1167
punakaikihotel@xtra.co.nz
à la carte hotel restaurant

The Smelting House Café
102 MacKay Street
Greymouth
03 768 0012
homestyle cooking in a converted bank

Café Nevé
Town Centre
Main Road
Fox Glacier
03 751 0110
cafe.neve@xtra.co.nz
fresh local ingredients

The Craypot
The Esplanade
Jackson Bay
Haast
03 750 0035
catches more than crayfish

Alfresco Outdoor Eatery & Pizzeria
16 Broadway
Reefton
03 732 8513
café food in a colonial garden

The Salmon Farm Café
State Highway 6
Paringa
South Westland
03 751 0837
fresh and smoked salmon dishes

Bushman's Café
The Bushman's Centre
Pukekura
State Highway 6
Lake Ianthe
South Westland
famous for wild foods, including venison and possum

that hide good numbers of medium to large trout. This is a remote wilderness fishery with no marked tracks, roads or huts, although anglers can fly into the upper reaches by helicopter. The Ohikanui offers fly fishers many opportunities to spot and stalk fish but you must be prepared to walk to reach the best water.

Buller River

The Buller reaches the sea at Westport after its long journey from the Nelson Lakes. Medium-sized sea-run brown trout are plentiful in the lower reaches in spring as they enter the river during whitebait season. Road access is good to both banks. Fly fishing is most productive at evening when trout feed near the surface on hatching nymphs. Side braids, shallow runs and the edges may be fished with a heavier nymph.

Inangahua River

The Inangahua River flows through forest and farmland to the Buller River upstream of Westport. It is a medium to large river, generally clear with a slight brown tinge during freshes. The Inangahua contains a very good population of trout, mainly medium- to small-sized but some in the 2–3 kg range, particularly late season.

The best fishing is in the middle reaches, both above and below Reefton. Above Reefton, SH7 follows close to the true right of the river and there are many places where there is easy access from the side of the road. There are few takeable fish in the upper section. Below Reefton landowner permission is mostly required although there are some places where 'access has been negotiated' signs have been erected. The mid-section around the Stony confluence is most suited to a heavy nymph fished near the edges. A large dry fly in any popular pattern will often produce a fish from the deeper runs.

Waitahu River

This is the largest of the Inangahua River tributaries and is about 4.5 km north of Reefton along SH69. It is an excellent stalk-and-fish river in a particularly scenic setting. There are trout all along the river which is best suited to fly fishing. Heavy nymph in deeper runs is most effective.

Awarau (Larrys) River

Another tributary of the Inangahua, about 15 km north of Reefton along SH69, Larrys contains trophy brown trout of 2–4 kg. As with the Waitahu River, fishing is good all season but during summer low-flows the required skill level increases.

RIVERS SOUTH OF GREYMOUTH

Taramakau River

There is good access to most of the Taramakau from SH73. It holds brown trout throughout with rainbows in the headwaters. The stretch of river between Jacksons and Kumara is ideal for quick stops.

Hokitika River

The lower reaches, which are usually well stocked with 1–2 kg browns and sea-runners early season, are easy to get to. The middle reaches are accessible off Kokatahi Road which leads through Kowhitirangi to the Hokitika Gorge. Rainbows are present in the upper reaches and in the Whitcombe tributary, one to two hours' walk from the road end. Accessible mid-section tributaries include the Kokatahi, Styx and Toaroha Rivers.

Murray and Harris Creeks

Smaller springfed streams accessible from Kokatahi–Kowhitirangi Road. Brown trout between 1–3 kg are typical. Catch and release is recommended.

Mahinapua Creek

Enters the Hokitika near the mouth on the south side. The best access is via Golf Links Road. Good early season fishing for sea-run browns, especially when main river is in flood.

Mikonui River

The lower reaches are best for the casual angler. Easy access can be had to the tidal portion at the SH6 bridge.

WHEN THE FISH DON'T BITE

Alpine Guides Fox Glacier
Main Road
Fox Glacier
03 751 0825
foxguides@minidata.co.nz
www.foxguides.co.nz
guided glacier walks

Franz Josef Glacier Guides
Main Road
Franz Josef
0800 484 337
03 752 0763
walks@franzjosefglacier.co.nz
www.franzjosefglacier.co.nz
walk through spectacular icefalls

Dragon's Cave Rafting
Clifton Road
Greymouth
03 768 9149
res@newzealandholiday.co.nz
raft through West Coast caves

Glacier Southern Lakes
Helicopters
Main Road
Fox Glacier
03 751 0803
fox@glaciersouthernlakes.co.nz
sample the glaciers effortlessly

Shantytown
Rutherglen Road
Greymouth
03 762 6649
shantytown@xtra.co.nz
www.shantytown.co.nz
1860s replica gold-mining town

Waitaha River

The section of river from the mouth to 2–3 km below SH6 is best. Turn west at the north end of the main road bridge.

Wanganui River

The lower reaches are best, with access via Wanganui Flat Road (turn off at Harihari); holds brown trout.

Poerua River

The best water is downstream of SH6. Peterson Road (turn off at Harihari) follows the lower river giving access to good fishing for sea-run browns.

La Fontaine Stream

A delightful springfed tributary of the Wanganui River. Access is available at various marked points off La Fontaine Road (turn off at Harihari). The upper section is accessible off Peterson Road. If in doubt about access ask at nearest farmhouse. An abundance of brown trout around 1–3 kg but can be challenging for inexperienced anglers.

Waitangitaona River

A medium-sized river which flows crystal clear in normal conditions. Good trout numbers in the lower section which is easily reached from the Lower Whataroa Flat Road – turn off at Whataroa and follow the signs to the 'White Heron Sanctuary Tours' boat launching ramp. There is about 4–5km of good water above and below this point.

Okarito River

The Okarito has a good brown trout population from December to March. Access is difficult because of the forest terrain but is easiest near the source at the Lake Mapourika outlet and near the Zalas Creek confluence, 15-minute drive from Franz Josef.

FURTHER SOUTH

Recommended rivers further south include the Paringa, Jacobs, Okuru, Turnbull and Jacksons. Most major river mouths and estuarine areas in South Westland fish well for sea-run browns during spring and early summer. Feathered lures representing whitebait, smelt and other forage fish are effective. Access to upper and lower sections of most rivers south of Fox Glacier is complex and usually only possible with the benefit of local advice.

WHEN THE FISH DON'T BITE

Wild West Adventure Company
8 Whall Street
Greymouth
0508 286 877
info@newzealandholiday.co.nz
whitewater rafting – beginners up to grade 5

Monteith's Brewing Company
cnr Turumaha and Herbert Streets
Greymouth
03 768 4149
info@monteiths.co.nz
www.monteiths.co.nz
home of the next best thing to gold

Jungle Boat Rainforest Cruise
8 Whall Street
Greymouth
03 768 9149
cruise@newzealandholiday.co.nz
float along the greenstone pathway

Above: Lake Taupo trout are mostly taken by trolling but in the Western Bays there is good shoreline fishing wherever streams run into the lake.

Below: The river that had Zane Grey drooling in the 1920s, the mighty Tongariro, still yields handsome catches in the Taupo region.

Left: One of New Zealand's most distinctive buildings, the Beehive, is part of the parliamentary complex in the country's capital city of Wellington.

Below: The Hutt River is a productive trout fishery near the heart of Wellington.

Above: The Travers River runs through the Travers Valley of Nelson Lakes National Park and offers superb wilderness fishing. DoC has built good tracks, bridges and huts that anglers can use.

Below: The upper Buller River (Nelson/Marlborough region) is such an important pristine fishery that it carries a National Water Conservation Order. Its clear waters also hold a lot of fine trout.

WWW.HURUNUI.COM

CANTERBURY MARKETING

Above: Pretty Hanmer Springs in North Canterbury is central to such excellent trout rivers as the Acheron, Clarence and Waiau.

Left: There is no better way to get the lie of the rivers running from the Southern Alps across the Canterbury Plains than by going aloft in a hot air balloon.

Opposite Above: Temple Stream near Lake Ohau, in the Central South Island region, is a fast-flowing mountain torrent that offers a great angling challenge.

Opposite: A 4.5kg North Canterbury brown caught – and released – just 200 m from the side of the road.

Left: Shoreline fishing among the weeds on Lake Brunner, one of the most popular spots in the West Coast region.

Left Below: Franz Josef Glacier's river of ice drops 2500 m in about 13 km before grinding to a halt just 10 km from the pounding surf of the Tasman Sea (West Coast region).

Opposite: The Kawarau River (Otago region) drains Lake Wakatipu and is a popular venue for extreme sports such as jet boating and bungy jumping.

Opposite Below: The streams and rivers flowing into Lake Wanaka provide some of the best fishing in Otago.

Above: The tree stumps on drowned Lake Monowai (Southland region) may be silent sentinels to the demands of the hydroelectric power generation, but the lake trout don't seem to mind.

Below: A seal colony on the Catlins Coast, an untouched corner of Southland that is home to an abundance of wildlife.

Central South Island

Trout fishing in New Zealand has a number of iconic images – a picket fence of fishers at a Lake Taupo stream mouth, a fighting trout bending a rod in a bush-fringed pool, and a line-up of nymph fishers on the Tongariro River. But the most truly spectacular image is surely that of an angler in a high-country stream set against the backdrop of the majestic snowclad peaks of the Southern Alps – a majestic idyll that sets trout fishing apart from every other type of fishing, and asserts that here is a pursuit staged in the grandest of outdoor amphitheatres, a pursuit that requires both skill and effort, and one which embraces a type of angling that is as far removed from dangling a line off the end of a wharf as the lofty Southern mountains are from a subtropical Northland beach.

The image is also emblematic of trout fishing in Fish and Game New Zealand's Central South Island region. This region embraces an area of New Zealand that seems designed by a gifted artist and certainly draws a host of them to it. The mountains provide a soaring backdrop and tussock-clad hills dominate the foreground. But that is just the sketchpad outline – it is the colours that truly set this region apart; subtle and forever changing colours. The mountain palette comprises every shade of blue, mauve and purple, the

FAMOUS FOR

- Moeraki Boulders
- Yellow-eyed penguins
- Gliding records
- Waitaki whitestone
- Aoraki-Mt Cook

- McKenzie Country
- Mountains
- Lake Tekapo
- Richard Pearse

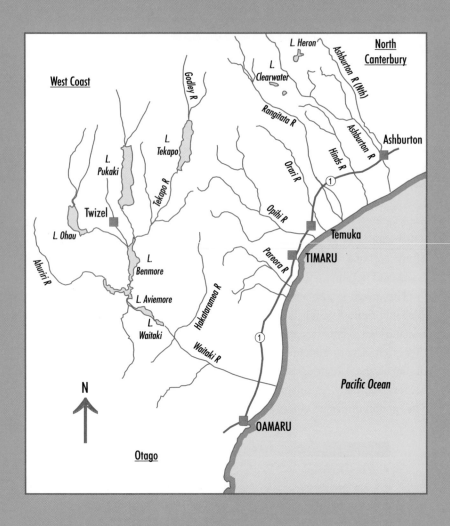

tussocks shimmer with the golds and russets of autumn, and the lakes are aquamarine, turquoise and milky blue with glacial flour. It is a magical landscape – and it is home to a trout fishery which as subtle and captivating as the district's colourings.

There are some large rivers in the region, but it is stalking brown trout in small streams that the Central South Island is most noted for. Sublime fishing in a sublime setting, and much to do besides fishing, although just to sit and stare is hard to beat. A place for artists, poets – and trout fishers.

INFORMATION

Fish and Game New Zealand Central South Island region
32 Richard Pearce Drive
Temuka
PO Box 150
Temuka
03 615 8400
csifgc@xtra.co.nz
www.fishandgame.org.nz
Manager: Jay Graybill
Field officers: Graeme Hughes, Graham McClintock, Mark Webb, Vaughan Lynn

Oamaru Visitor Information Centre
1 Thames Street
Oamaru
03 434 1656
info@tourismwaitaki.co.nz
www.tourismwaitaki.co.nz

National Park Visitor Centre
Mt Cook Village
03 435 1186
mtcookvc@doc.govt.nz

Timaru Visitor Information Centre
14 George Street
Timaru
03 688 6163
www.southisland.org.nz

Geraldine Visitor Information Centre
Talbot Street
Geraldine
03 693 1006
Geraldine_info@xtra.co.nz

Ashburton Visitor Information Centre
East Street
Ashburton
03 308 1050
www.adt.co.nz

WHERE AND WHAT

Fish and Game New Zealand's Central South Island region extends from the south bank of the Rakaia River in the north, to Moeraki in the south. With their headwaters in the Southern Alps, the Waitaki and the Rangitata are the region's biggest rivers, and are noted Chinook salmon fisheries with trophy fish of 15 kg and more being regularly reported. Lesser rivers include the Opihi-Temuka, Ashburton and Kakanui, which, together with many high-country lakes, are habitat to substantial brown and rainbow trout fisheries. Sockeye salmon and *fontinalis* (brook char) add further variety for the keen angler. In fact, this region offers some of the best wilderness angling waters in the country.

The Central South Island's regulations follow the general South Island regulations, and for most waters in the region the fishing season runs from 1 October to 30 April.

On the Ahuriri River Lagoons and the river's tributaries upstream of and including Longslip Creek, the season is from 1 December to 30 April; on the Ashburton River (south branch) and Bowyers Stream from 1 October to 31 March; on Lake Camp from 3 November to 31 May; on Lake Stream from 1 October to 28 February; and on Larch Stream from 3 November to 31 January.

The season on Lakes Poaka, Merino, Macgregor, Alexandrina, the Ashburton Lakes, Cameron Loch, Deep Stream and the Otematata River and its tributaries is from 3 November to 30 April.

The Rangitata diversion from the intake downstream to Rakaia River Road, Tekapo River downstream from Lake Benmore, Upper Waitaki Lakes and Waitaki hydro canals, are open all year.

Fishing is restricted to fly fishing only on the Ahuriri River Lagoons, Maerewhenua, Tengawai, Hinds, and Hakataramea Rivers, all high-country tarns, Maori Lakes, Cameron Loch, Lakes Merino, Denny, Donn, Poaka, Emily, Roundabout and Spider, and the Ohapi, Omarama, and Deep Streams.

In most of the region the daily bag limit is four trout but a limit of two trout applies to most upland lakes, rivers, tarns and streams, and the upper reaches of the region's rivers.

Casting 🎣 around

ASHBURTON RIVER

One of our smaller salmon rivers, the Ashburton River mouth is popular with trout anglers looking for sea-run browns early in the season. The mouth is reached from the Hakatere Huts on the north bank. A number of ford crossings give access to the main river and its two principal branches; the North Ashburton and South Ashburton Rivers. On the former, good fishing water is available upstream from SH72, and for the latter, upstream from the junction of Taylors Stream at Valetta.

RANGITATA RIVER

The Rangitata River is famous for its salmon fishery. Its headwaters are high in the Southern Alps and it is prone to floods and freshes from high rainfall and snowmelt. The Rangitata is also noted for its sea-run brown trout early in the season.

WAITAKI RIVER

Second only in flow to the Clutha River to the south, the Waitaki is widely recognised for its magnificent salmon and trout fisheries. Modified by extensive hydroelectric power development over the last 60 years, the Waitaki and its extensive hydro lakes and canals provide quality fishing.

WAITAKI RIVER TRIBUTARIES

Hakataramea River

The Hakataramea River has both brown and rainbow trout and is restricted to fly fishing only. Best access is from McHenrys Road, which follows the river for about 12 km to Wrights Crossing. Above Wrights Crossing, road access is available only along the west side of the river to its upper reaches above Cattle Creek. Except for a short section above Cattle Creek there are

149

no marginal strips and landowner permission is required to cross land to reach the river.

Ahuriri River

The Ahuriri River flows into the Ahuriri Arm of Lake Benmore near Omarama. It is most scenic in the upper reaches where trophy trout await the attention of experienced anglers. The Ahuriri River has long been considered a fishery of national importance and enjoys 'Water Conservation Order' status. Upstream from Omarama access is from SH8 or from Birchwood Road, which branches off SH8 17 km south of Omarama. The pristine upper river waters can be reached directly from Birchwood Road, or alternatively at Irelands Bridge or by walking down the Avon Burn.

Downstream from Omarama the north side of the Ahuriri River may be accessed from Ben Omar Road, which turns off just over the SH8 bridge. The Ahuriri delta with Lake Benmore is best reached through Glenburn Station via an anglers' access track located about 5.5 km from Omarama along SH83. A 20-minute walk from the end of the track takes you to the river mouth.

Tekapo River

The Tekapo River is harnessed for hydro power generation but its flow is augmented by Fork Stream, Grays River, and the Mary Burn, and arguably it produces more fish than any other river of the region. The river is reached from the Tekapo Canal Road, which turns off SH8 1.5 km south of the Tekapo township.

Orari River

This river supports the occasional run of salmon but is mainly noted for its brown trout fishing within the lower reaches below Rolleston Road. Ohapi Creek is a

TACKLE BOX

Dix's Firearms & Fishing Centre
26 Canon Street
Timaru
03 688 3728

Wilson's Sports Centre
223 Thames Street
Oamaru
03 434 8231

Falconers Field & Stream Sports
39 King Street
Timaru
03 684 6631

Temuka Fishing & Shooting Centre
135 King Street
Temuka
03 615 7496

GUIDES AND CHARTERS

Back Country Trout
Gudex Road
Cattle Flat
Fairlie
03 614 7107

Lloyd Knowles
Earnscleugh Road
RD1 Clyde
03 449 2122

Sedge Creek
PO Box 32
Oamaru
03 431 7794
driftboat@xtra.co.nz
www.sedgecreek.co.nz

Brian Minty
17 Awamoa Road
Oamaru
03 434 7105
bminty@xtra.co.nz

Eric Prattley
Wallingford Road
Temuka
03 615 9386

Kevin Payne
20 Murray Street
Temuka
03 615 6101
kevin.jodi@xtra.co.nz

Barry Sinclair
11 Lismore Street
Oamaru
03 437 1750

springfed stream and enters the Orari about 1 km above the mouth. About 5 m wide and 0.5 m deep, the Ohapi provides good spotting water for the fly angler, but is bounded on both banks by private land so the landowners' permission is required – they are usually quite receptive to angler requests.

Opihi River

This river supports a good population of brown trout, and along with its main branches – the Temuka and the Waihi – is popular with anglers. These rivers may be accessed at any number of points; for the Opihi, the more popular being at Milford Huts, Wareing Road and SH1 on the north bank; and Waipopo Huts, Seadown Road, Roaring Camp Road, Saleyards Bridge (Pleasant Point), Hanging Rock Bridge and Raincliff Bridge, on the south side; for the Temuka/Waihi system, SH1, SH72 and Coach Road are the favoured access sites.

Best fishing is from the mouth of the Opihi up to SH1. Also try the Waihi above Winchester, the Te Ngawai above Pleasant Point – particularly early in the season – and the Opihi around the Hanging Rock Bridge.

Pareora River

The Pareora is mainly noted for its sea-run browns early in the season when river flows are elevated following the spring thaw. From December onwards the river suffers from low flows, made more extreme by irrigation draw-off.

151

Best access is from the Pareora River Road that follows up the south side.

Waihao River

One of our smaller rivers, this is nonetheless a little gem for brown trout anglers. There is good fishing at the mouth, from the 'Box' upstream to Bradshaws Bridge; upstream the willow-lined banks and tranquil deep pools of the lower gorge provide a nice change from the typical braided river. Unfortunately, access is limited to only two points – where Gum Tree Flat Road meets the river, and at McCulloughs Bridge.

ASHBURTON LAKES

The popularity of the Ashburton Lakes, nestled between the Rakaia and Rangitata Rivers, has spawned a fishing village between Lakes Camp and Clearwater. The area is reached from Mt Somers township via the Ashburton Gorge Road. At the Hakatere Corner (23 km from Mt Somers), the road branches – right to Maori Lakes and Lake Heron, and straight ahead to Spider Lakes and Lakes Clearwater, Camp, Emma, and Roundabout.

GUIDES AND CHARTERS

Dick Marquand
PO Box 32
Cromwell
03 445 1745
dick@troutfishingservices.co.nz
www.nzsouth.co.nz/troutfishing

Kenneth McGraw
17 Pisa Moorings Road
Lowburn
Cromwell
03 445 0516
wild.trout@xtra.co.nz

Steven Carey
Aoraki Lodge
Twizel
03 435 0300
aorakilodge@xtra.co.nz
www.fishnhunt.co.nz/trout/carey

Frank Schlosser
PO Box 143
Lake Tekapo
03 680 6797
murrayriver@xtra.co.nz

Max Irons
9 Black Peak Road
Omarama
03 438 9468
maxfishing@xtra.co.nz

Grant Brown
36 Murray Place
Lake Tekapo
03 680 6516
GrantBrown@xtra.co.nz

Lake Heron

Lake Heron, 15 km from the Hakatere Corner, is the largest of the lakes and is home to good populations of brown and rainbow trout. There is also the odd landlocked quinnat salmon. Rowboats and canoes may be used to fish, but beware of the nor'wester which may quickly chop up the lake.

Maori Lakes, bypassed on the way to Lake Heron, are surrounded by wetland and raupo swamp. Fishing from anchored rowboats is permitted.

Lakes Roundabout, Emma, and the Spider Lakes

On the road to Lake Clearwater, 5 km from the Hakatere Corner, a signpost marks the gate and vehicle track to Lakes Roundabout and Emma. On the opposite side of the road, 4 km from the Corner, there is a track which leads off to Spider Lakes – a short 1 km walk is necessary if the track is muddy. Fishing from a moored rowboat is permitted on Lake Emma, however boats are prohibited on Lake Roundabout and the Spider Lakes.

Lake Camp

Lake Camp, 9 km from the Corner, is the only lake where powerboating is permitted. Swimming, boating, and water-skiing activities tend to dominate, but during quiet periods the odd quality rainbow often rewards angler effort.

Lake Clearwater

In comparison, Lake Clearwater is a place of relative peace and solitude. This scenic lake with its picturesque fishing village is 10 km from the Haketere Corner. The lake is open to both fly and spin fishing. While fishing from an anchored rowboat is permitted, most anglers prefer to walk the lake margins stalking the cruising browns with polaroids and an accurate cast. To reach the northern side away from the prevailing nor'westers, drive past the village about 2 km to the head of the lake and walk from there.

WAITAKI BASIN LAKES

Lake Alexandrina

From Tekapo township, 2 km south and AA signposted, the Godley Peaks Road will take you to Lake Alexandrina. Much smaller than Lake Tekapo, Alexandrina has long been considered the most productive of the lakes in the area. Tony Orman credits the lake as one of the best trout-fishing waters in the country. It has produced browns of over 6 kg.

To reach the southern end, a side road leaves Godley Peaks Road about

HANG YOUR HOOK

The Hermitage
Aoraki/Mt Cook National Park
03 435 1809
reservations.hermitage@xtra.co.nz
classic accommodation in a sublime setting

Oakbridge Holidaystay
McPhersons Road
Waitaki Bridge
Oamaru
03 431 3736
info@tourismwaitaki.co.nz
www.tourismwaitaki.co.nz
restored country school

Tokarahi Homestead
47 Dip Hill Road
Tokarahi
Oamaru
03 431 2500
tokarahi@xtra.co.nz
www.homestead.co.nz
elegance in restored 1870s limestone cottage

Rivendell Lodge
Stanton Road
Kimbell
RD17 Fairlie
03 685 8833
rivendell.lodge@xtra.co.nz
www.fairlie.co.nz/rivendell
take time out to relax in a haven of peace

Tighnafeile House
62 Wai-iti Road
Timaru
03 684 3333
Tighnafeile-house@timaru.co.nz
the name is Gaelic for 'House of Welcome'

Creel House B&B
36 Murray Place
Lake Tekapo
03 680 6516
Creelhouse.1.tek@xtra.co.nz
guided fly fishing trips a highlight

Lake Tekapo Lodge
24 Aorangi Crescent
Lake Tekapo
03 680 6566
lake.tekapo.lodge@xtra.co.nz
www.laketekapolodge.co.nz
one of the most stunning views in the world

The Godley Resort Hotel
State Highway 8
Lake Tekapo
03 680 6848
info@tekapo.co.nz
www.thegodley.com
breathtaking views of the lake and surrounding mountains

Aoraki Lodge
32 Mackenzie Drive
Twizel
03 435 0300
aorakilodge@xtra.co.nz
professional fishing guide host

Mountain Chalet Motels
Wairepo Road
Twizel
03 435 0785
mt.chalets@xtra.co.nz
magnificent views of Mt Cook

The Crossing
Woodbury Road
RD21
Geraldine
03 693 9689
srelax@xtra.co.nz
fully licensed bar and à la carte restaurant

Heritage Gateway Hotel
State Highway 8
Omarama
03 438 9805
heritagegateway@xtra.co.nz
in the heart of the Mt Cook fishing region

3.5 km from the SH8 turn-off. To reach the middle of the lake, continue a further 5 km and turn left past Lake McGregor to the outlet and fishing huts. To reach the northern end of the lake, return to Godley Peaks Road and drive to Glenmore Station, 5 km from Lake McGregor. A track through deer paddocks then leads to the huts near the lake shore.

Anglers are able to walk and fish from well-worn tracks around the lake edge using either spinning or fly fishing techniques. Rowboats are permitted on Lake Alexandrina but must be moored when fishing Lake McGregor.

WAITAKI HYDRO LAKES

Well known to South Island anglers, Lakes Waitaki, Aviemore, and Benmore cater for thousands of anglers every year. All are easily accessible by good

CATCH A MEAL

Golden Dragon Chinese Restaurant
36–38 Ribble Street
Oamaru
03 434 8670
Chinese cuisine

Merino Country Café
State Highway 83
Omarama
03 438 9844
traditional fare

Whitestone Cheese Factory and Café
3 Torridge Street
Oamaru
03 434 8098
wstonecheese@xtra.co.nz
blackboard menu

Kavanagh House
State Highway 1
Winchester
03 615 6150
country food with flair

Armada Motor Inn
500 Thames Highway
Oamaru
03 437 0017
www.armadagalleon.com
armada.galleon@xtra.co.nz
family restaurant pizza and stone-grill

Golden Island Chinese Restaurant
243 Thames Street
Oamaru
03 434 8840
Chinese cuisine

The Last Post Pub Restaurant
12 Thames Street
Oamaru
03 434 8080
pub meals

Harbourside Café
No. 1 Wharf
Timaru
03 684 4744
seafood

roads, have facilities for camping, and are serviced by Kurow, Otematata and Omarama townships.

State Highway 83 from Kurow to Omarama provides angler access to the south side of Lakes Waitaki, Aviemore, and the Ahuriri Arm of Lake Benmore. There is no road access on the northern side of the Ahuriri Arm. The Haldon Arm of Lake Benmore can be reached by boat from the Ahuriri Arm – if driving however, it will mean a trip to Twizel turning off at the Ruataniwha spillway and driving alongside the hydro canal to Ohau 'C' power station. A metalled road continues around the southern shoreline of the lake for about 12 km. The Haldon Arm can also be accessed via the Haldon Road, which branches off SH8, 2 km south of Burkes Pass.

WHEN THE FISH DON'T BITE

Coast Line Tours
135 Newlands Road
Oamaru
03 439 5265
coastline@hyper.net.nz
www.tourismwaitaki.co.nz
explore the coastline

Oamaru Blue Penguin Colony
Waterfront Road
Oamaru
03 433 1195
obpc@penguin.net.nz
www.tourismwaitaki.co.nz
watch the world's smallest penguin at play

Oamaru Bushy Beach Yellow-Eyed
Penguin Tours
38 Glendale Crescent
Oamaru
03 434 6033
penguin watch

Rangitata Rafts
Peel Forest
RD20 South Canterbury
0800 251 251
raft exciting white water

Mount Cook Skiplanes
Mount Cook Airport
03 435 1026
mtcook@skiplanes.co.nz
www.skiplanes.co.nz
land on the Tasman Glacier

High Country Tours
Visitor Information Centre
Landing Service Building
George Street
Timaru
03 688 6163
guided tours of some best-kept secrets

Timaru Marine Cruises
No. 1 Wharf
Port of Timaru
Timaru
03 688 6881
see a diverse range of marine wildlife

The Wool Store
1 Tyne Street
Harbourside
Oamaru
03 434 1556
historic surroundings

Otago

Trout fishing in the South Island is quite distinct from that in the North Island. The country that feeds the streams, rivers and lakes is noticeably different in the two islands. The trout are different too, with rainbows predominating in the North Island and browns in South Island waters. The exception to the general rule that divides New Zealand trout fishing into two distinct types separated by Cook Strait, is the Taupo fishery which, because it is centred on a huge lake, tends to sustain itself without much influence from either mountains or men.

The one region in the South Island that comes closest to replicating the unique Taupo ecology is Otago. Its main rivers rise in alpine high country and flow into the Pacific, as do those in the Central South Island region to the north. The key difference is that Otago has several major lakes in which its waters collect before heading for the ocean. That means the region can offer good lake-style fishing. It also means that the region divides into two parts. There are superb high-country wilderness rivers and streams that are used by fish from the lakes for spawning. Many of these rivers contain some of the clearest water in the world where rainbow and brown trout are easy to spot but are not always so easy to catch. And then there are big river fisheries with trout moving from the sea mouths and coastal estuaries.

The region includes three renowned trout-fishing waters. The Makarora River, which has its headwaters in the Southern Alps near Mt Brewster, is a wonderful river valley fishery crowded in by snowcapped mountains and beech forest before opening into tussock flats as the river enters Lake Wanaka. There is a lifetime of wilderness fishing just on the Makarora and its

157

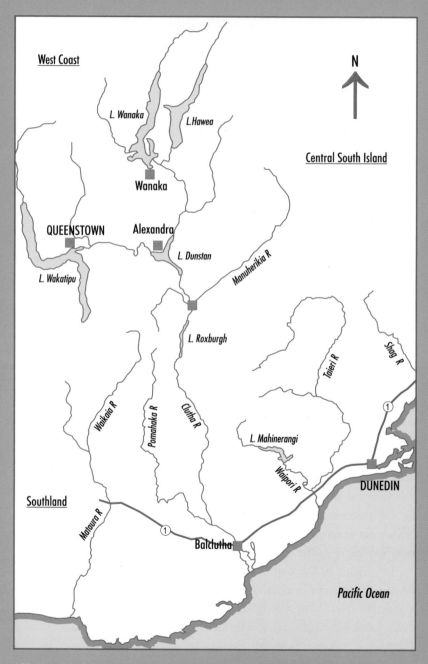

tributaries. The upper reaches of the Clutha River, which drains Lake Wanaka, is considered by many to offer the best dry fly fishing water you will find in the summer twilight of the South Island. And Lake Dunstan, into which the upper Clutha flows and builds up behind the Clyde Dam, is a lake where trout relish the abundance of food and grow to trophy size.

The southern lakes, lying in the paths of ancient glaciers, are at the heart of New Zealand's reputation for outdoor recreation, with Wanaka and Queenstown – both in spectacular Southern Alps settings – vying to be the capital. In the winter they share four downhill ski and snowboard areas, and the major heli-skiing operations in the country. In the summer they become Otago's aquatic playground. There is a plethora of accommodation choice and fine restaurants. And there are plenty of magnificent trout.

INFORMATION

Fish and Game New Zealand Otago region
40 Hanover Street
PO Box 76
Dunedin
03 477 9076
s.kyle@fish-game.org.nz/otago
www.fishandgame.org.nz
Manager: Niall Watson
Regional Officers:
Monty Wright (North Coast/Maniototo)
03 479 6555
Richard Fitzpatrick (South/West Otago)
03 479 6556
Tom Kroos (Queenstown) 03 441 8583
Cliff Halford (Wanaka) 03 443 7893

Queenstown Travel and Visitor Information Centre
Clocktower Centre
cnr Shotover and Camp Streets
03 442 4100
qvc@xtra.co.nz
www.newzealand-vacation.com

Destination Queenstown
44 Stanley Street
Queenstown
03 442 7440
queenstown@xtra.co.nz
www.queenstown-nz.co.nz

Wanaka Visitor Information Centre
Ardmore Street
Wanaka
03 443 1233
www.wanaka.co.nz

Dunedin Visitor Information Centre
48 The Octagon
Dunedin
03 474 3300
www.cityofdunedin.com

Central Otago Visitor Information Centre
22 Centennial Ave
Alexandra
03 448 9515
info@tco.org.nz

On the coast Dunedin, the Otago capital, is the home of the university 'scarfies' and the 'House of Pain' – the Highlanders' celebrated rugby stadium – yet always displays its sedate Scottish ancestry. Dunedin is anything but brash, and that is its appeal – for a weekend or a week. When you stay in Dunedin make sure you pack a trout rod; the mouth of Leith Stream in the central city is worth a dabble for sea-run trout and the city's water supply reservoirs are restocked every year and open to fishing all year round.

WHERE AND WHAT

Fish and Game New Zealand's Otago region extends from Shag Point on the South Island's east coast south to The Brothers Point in the Catlins area. The region runs inland to include the whole of both the Clutha and Taieri River catchments as well as a number of smaller coastal river catchments such as the Catlins, Tahakopa, Tokomairiro, Kaikorai, Waitati, Waikouaiti and Shag.

The region has small still-water fisheries ranging from Dunedin city's water supply reservoirs to coastal lakes such Waihola, Waipori and Tuakitoto that hold brown trout. Coastal estuaries and tidal river reaches on the Waikouaiti, Taieri, Tokomairiro, Clutha and Catlins Rivers all have good numbers of sea-run and resident brown trout. The larger electricity and irrigation reservoirs in Central Otago are good for lake-style fishing but the two major lake fisheries in Otago are Lake Wanaka and Lake Wakatipu.

The region's regulations follow the general South Island sports fishing regulations. Most waters in Otago are open to fishing all year round. There is a closed season from 31 May to 1 October on the Arrow, Lindis and Shotover Rivers, Lakes Mahinerangi, and Kirkpatrick, and Diamond Creek. The Nevis River is closed between 30 April and 1 October; the rivers and streams flowing into Lake Mahinerangi

from 30 April to 1 October; and the rivers and streams flowing into Lake Dunstan, the Upper Manorburn Dam and Lakes Hawea, Wakatipu and Wanaka, from 31 May until 1 November.

There are fly fishing only restrictions on the upper section of the Clutha River, the Nevis and Route Burn Rivers, and all rivers and streams flowing into Lake Wakatipu except the Dart and the Rees.

The daily bag limit is one trout on rivers flowing into Lakes Hawea, Wanaka and Wakatipu, Manuherikia River above Beck's Bridge, Nevis River, Southern Reservoir, Sullivans Dam, Upper Tomahawk Lagoon, Fraser River, and Von Lake. A daily limit of three trout applies to Coalpit , Hoffmans, and Mathias Dams; Diamond, Kirkpatrick, and Reids Lakes; and the upper reaches of the Pomahaka River. In other waters the daily limit is six.

Anglers have good access to most Otago waterways, often with landowner goodwill. Sometimes access through private property is temporarily closed, such as during lambing season, and anglers should respect the restrictions. In addition to signposted access points there are hundreds of others where permission to pass through private land will be readily given to the angler who takes the trouble to ask.

Special publications

The Otago region has an excellent guidebook, *The Guide to Trout Fishing in Otago*, which covers 140 waters throughout Otago (including Waitaki Valley and Eastern Southland). Available from the Fish and Game New Zealand Otago region office, this 128-page book gives good information on access, the best angling methods to use, and the best times of the year to use them. The guide retails for $19.95 plus $2 for postage and packaging. Maps and brochures for several waters are available free from most tackle shops.

Casting  around

DUNEDIN CITY

Sullivan's Dam, Southern Reservoir (both water supply reservoirs) and Tomahawk Lagoon are stocked each year with trout. The water reservoirs are open all year round and anglers can use fly or spinning methods. The mouth of Leith Stream in the central city is a popular spot for spin anglers.

NORTH OTAGO

Shag River

A medium-sized river with its headwaters in the Kakanui Mountains. There are few pools that hold trout in the upper reaches, but from Dunback to the mouth at Shag Point, near Palmerston, there are good numbers of fish up to 2.5 kg. In summer fish can be spotted in the clear, slow-moving water and stalked with dry fly and nymph. Sea-run trout are found in the lower reaches and estuary when whitebait are running. Landowner permission is needed for access to much of the river.

Waikouaiti River

This river, which has its source in tussock-covered hills west of Waikouaiti, offers similar fishing to the Shag. There are sea-run trout near the mouth that take smelt flies, and fly fishing for the energetic angler in the upper reaches.

SOUTH OTAGO

Taieri River

The Taieri reaches the sea south of Dunedin after a 250 km journey from the Central Otago high country. From the headwaters to Waipiata the river is slow and convoluted and fishing is generally unproductive in the peat-stained water. However, in the gorge at Hore's Bridge there are deep pools which hold some good-sized brown trout that respond to dry fly and nymphs. Between Waipiata and Kokonga the river is easily accessible and offers good fly fishing. Between Hyde and Sutton the river flows over a shingle bed and the fly fishing is reasonable. In the lower reaches from Outram to the mouth the fishing is generally difficult but sea-run trout are caught at the mouth from September to November on smelt imitation flies.

Deep Stream

A Taieri River tributary that joins the Taieri above Hindon. The water is peat-stained and has boulders, rock reefs and stones as its bed. Dry fly and nymph fishing is successful throughout the season.

Lower Waipori River

In the Waipori Gorge the river holds good brown trout in attractive bush surroundings. Fly fishing is effective. Below the gorge the river is tidal and uninteresting, although it does hold trout.

Lower Clutha River

Between Clyde and Alexandra this large and swift river becomes difficult to fish but below Balclutha, where it divides into two branches, good catches are taken all year round. In summer the tidal reaches yield large sea-run trout to smelt lures.

Waiwera River

Drains the Kaihiku Range and joins the Clutha downstream from Clydevale. Access is mostly across farmland and landowner permission is required. The upper reaches have good water holding browns of around 1 kg that respond to weighted nymphs or dry flies. It is best fished early in the season.

Pomahaka River

Rises in the Umbrella Mountains south of Roxburgh and winds for 125 km through West Otago to enter the Clutha below Clydevale not far from the mouth of the Waiwera river. There's good road access to most of the river. Fish can be spotted in the clear upper reaches which meander across exposed tussock country. During February and March sea-run browns from the Clutha weighing up to 4.5 kg spawn in this area and can be taken on nymphs, dry flies and black lures fished deep after dark. In the middle and lower reaches there is some boots-and-shorts fishing in Dusky Forest where good-sized fish are found when the river slows from Tapanui to Conical Hill.

Owaka River

The Owaka discolours easily after rain but holds trout up to 1.3 kg. Best fished early in the season.

Catlins River

The Catlins, a scenic river holding brown trout averaging up to 2 kg, can be hard to fish. The upper reaches are a test for anglers using dry fly or nymph, with fish difficult to spot in the tea-stained waters and casting difficult because the banks are covered in gorse. There are reasonable numbers of fish in the pools through the Catlins State Forest Park but the water must be fished blind. The river is better for fly fishing in the stretch around Franks Creek but most fish are taken on spinners. Near the mouth the tidal Catlins Lake holds sea-run trout that can be caught on spinners and smelt flies from a boat.

CENTRAL OTAGO

Lake Mahinerangi

A large exposed lake that holds brown and rainbow trout with easy fishing from the shoreline with dry fly.

Manuherikia River

The Manuherikia rises in the dry, tussock-covered St Bathans Range close to Lindis Pass and flows down the Manuherikia Valley to join the Clutha River at Alexandra. The middle and lower reaches can be low, warm and clear in summer and hard to fish. The best fishing is east of the historic gold-mining town of St Bathans, below Falls Dam.

Falls Dam

An irrigation dam in the headwaters of the Manuherikia River in lovely tussock country north of St Bathans. Most of the trout are fairly small but large fish are sometimes taken.

Coalpit Dam and Hoffmans Dam

These dams in the Naseby Forest near Naseby, are regularly stocked. Coalpit holds browns while Hoffmans has both rainbow and browns. Most fish are taken on nymphs and bully imitations.

Butchers Dam

A shallow lake with browns up to 1.2 kg. Fish cruise the shallow inlets and will take dry flies and nymphs.

Upper Manorburn Reservoir

A large, deep dam in bleak Central Otago that is exclusive to rainbows. There is little angling pressure and trout stocks are good with fish up to 1.5 kg. The Lower Manorburn Dam between Alexandra and Galloway holds small brown trout.

Lake Onslow

This large lake formed by damming the upper Teviot River is one of Otago's best still-water lakes. It is home to brown trout only which relish the lake's many spawning streams and reach up to 3.5 kg. At 700 m above sea level

GUIDES AND CHARTERS

Gavin Pegley
7 Henderson Street
Mornington
Dunedin
03 453 6679
gavin@encounters.co.nz

Tony Murphy
PO Box 1211
Queenstown
03 442 9656
Cast@tonymurphy.net.nz
www.tonymurphy.net.nz

Grant Alley
Frankton
Queenstown
03 442 9208
GrantAlley@xtra.co.nz
www.southerntrout.co.nz

Trevor Cruickshank
9B York Street
Queenstown
03 442 4462
FishingDiscovery@xtra.co.nz

Harvey Maguire
334 Littles Road
Queenstown
03 442 9088
harvey@flyfishing.net.nz
www.flyfishing.net.nz

GUIDES AND CHARTERS

Waitaki River Driftboat fishing
Jeff Jones
PO Box 624
Queenstown
03 442 6570
jeffjones@fishing.co.nz
www.fishing.co.nz

Arthur Gray
39 Matai Street
Wanaka
03 4437279
fishing.co.@xtra.co.nz
www.trout.net.nz

Gerald Telford
PO Box 312
Wanaka
03 443 9257
gtelfor@es.co.nz
www.flyfishhunt.co.nz

Richard Grimmett
37 Hunter Crescent
Wanaka
03 4437748
guide@trout.net.nz
www.trout.net.nz

Ian Cole
43 Russell Street
Wanaka
03 443 7870
IanCole@xtra.co.nz

and surrounded by high-country farmed tussock land, the lake has a distinctive atmosphere. There is good access to the west and north through either Millers Flat or Roxburgh. To reach the rest of the lake you need a boat or to be prepared to walk. Trolling is popular.

Teviot River

The Teviot drains into and out of Lake Onslow before joining the Clutha River at Roxburgh. It holds high stocks of small brown trout and can be fun to fish.

Loganburn Reservoir

A fairly new artificial lake that covers the Great Moss Swamp at the southern end of the Rock and Pillar Range west of Sutton. There are good numbers of brown trout that respond to dry and wet flies, spinners and terrestrial imitations, especially cicada, in summer.

LAKE WANAKA REGION

Makarora River

The Makarora drains the Young Range and flows down a wide tussock valley into Lake Wanaka south of Makarora. It holds browns and rainbows but is only suitable for fly fishing in the upper reaches above the confluence with the Young River. The lower, braided reaches are better for spin fishing although the fly fisher will be tempted to try the clear water at Cameron, Kiwi and Davis Flats. Access to the Makarora is good and limited stocks are under a lot of angling pressure.

Young River

The Young has mainly rainbow trout. It is mountain water with short deep pools and is challenging to fish. The best fishing spots require some tramping to get to.

Wilkin River

The Wilkin joins the Makarora about 9 km above Lake Wanaka. It runs through a typically beautiful South Island river valley of tussock flats, beech forest and snow-covered mountain backdrop. That makes it popular with anglers who like to mix tramping with fishing but it requires good outdoors skills – fording the river can be hazardous. The best fishing is in late summer when the water is low and clear. Fly fishers need to walk about 12 km upstream to reach good pools and runs overhung by beech trees that are best fished with weighted nymphs.

The Siberia Stream, which joins the Wilkin at Kerin Forks, also offers good fly fishing but it could be decimated unless catch-and-release is practised. There is a DoC hut at Kerin Forks.

Matukituki River

The Matukituki is fed from the snows of Mt Aspiring and surrounding mountains and flows into Lake Wanaka above Glendhu Bay. There is road access to the lower reaches and a 4WD track to the upper reaches as far as Aspiring Hut, although it is intended for emergency use only. The river holds browns and rainbows but this is wilderness fishing country and you need to be as interested in the magnificent scenery as in catch rates.

TACKLE BOX

Queenstown Sportsworld
17 Rees Street
Queenstown
03 442 8452

McCarthys Stream & Field Store
358 Moray Place
Dunedin
03 477 3266

Allan Millar's Hunting & Fishing
20 Manse Street
Dunedin
03 477 6665

Wazza's Fly Box
404 Taieri Road
Dunedin
03 476 6334

Brown Trout Fly & Tackle
cnr Albion Street & Main Garston Highway
Athol
Garston
03 248 8855

HANG YOUR HOOK

Larnach Lodge
145 Camp Road
Otago Peninsula
Dunedin
03 476 1616
larnarch@larnarchcastle.co.nz
*next to Larnarch Castle overlooking the
Otago Harbour*

Lisburn House
15 Lisburn Ave
Caversham
Dunedin
03 455 8888
stay@lisburnhouse.co.nz
cosy B&B in a Victorian gothic home

Fletcher Lodge
276 High Street
Dunedin
03 477 5552
lodge@es.co.nz
built by Sir James Fletcher for his own use

Corstorphine House
23A Milburn Street
Corstorphine
Dunedin
Corstorphine@globaladdress.com
www.corstorphine.co.nz
*Edwardian mansion built in 1863 on a hill
overlooking Dunedin*

Larchwood Lodge
Dublin Bay
RD2 Wanaka
03 443 7914
larchwood@xtra.co.nz
tranquil rural atmosphere

Oakridge Lake Wanaka
cnr Cardrona Valley and Studholme Roads
Wanaka
03 443 7707
info@oakridge.co.nz
purpose-built hunting, fishing and ski lodge

Montery Lodge
173 Camphill Road
Hawea Flat
Wanaka
03 443 1983
john.bill@xtra.co.nz
*facilities include rods so you can catch
brown and rainbow trout in the nearby river*

Constable Cottage and Gaol
Lauderdale
RD2 Omakau
Central Otago
03 447 3558
lauderdale@xtra.co.nz
*historic police cottage on the edge of Lake
Bathans*

Villa Sorgenfrei
11 ArrowtownLake Hayes Road
Queenstown
03 442 1128
villa@xtra.co.nz
*you can spot Lake Hayes trout from the
breakfast table*

Lakehouse Lodge
Arrowtown–Lake Hayes Road
RD1 Queenstown
03 442 1394
lakehouse.lodge@xtra.co.nz
www.lakehouse.co.nz
*private lake access to a secluded fishing
spot where trout are readily available*

Trelawn Place
Gorge Road
Arthurs Point
Queenstown
03 442 9160
trelawn@ihug.co.nz
www.trelawnb-b.co.nz
*host Michael Clark will guide you on trout-
fishing trips in the area*

Lake Wanaka

This large lake has brown and rainbow trout and landlocked quinnat salmon. Road access to the shore is limited and most fish are taken by trolling. As well, some of the best shoreline fishing spots can only be reached by boat. However, there is shoreline access from the road to Glendhu Bay and West Wanaka, and from SH6 on the eastern shore from the head of the lake to The Neck. There is also some access from the streets around the Wanaka township. Trout can be stalked cruising the shoreline. Spin fishing is popular and productive; Paddock Bay, reached off the West Wanaka Road, is a favoured fly fishing area. Stevensons Arm, the Makarora and Matukituki deltas and Glendhu Bay are popular for trolling.

Lake Hawea

The lake holds browns, rainbows and landlocked quinnat salmon that are mostly taken from a boat or by spin fishing from the shore. Trout cruising shallow bays respond to flies. The most popular spots are The Neck, the mouth of Timaru Creek, the Hunter River delta, the Dingle Burn delta and Silver Island.

Hunter River

A large river with its headwaters in the Bealey Range that drains into Lake Hawea with a reputation as a premier trout fishery. Access is mainly by jet-boat. Although there is wet fly and spin fishing in the lower reaches, the energetic wilderness angler prepared to put in many hours of tramping will be rewarded with superb dry fly and nymph fishing in the upper reaches.

HANG YOUR HOOK

The Dairy Guesthouse
10 Isle Street
Queenstown
03 442 5164
thedairy@xtra.co.nz
*super-cosy award-winning
midtown accommodation*

Driftwood
PO Box 2176
Wakatipu
Queenstown
03 442 7088
info@driftwood.net.nz
www.driftwood.net.nz
*secluded lakeside retreat nestled
in native bush beneath The
Remarkables*

**Mataura Valley Station
Farmstay Fishing Lodge**
Cainard Road
Garston
Queenstown–Te Anau Highway
03 248 8552
matauravalley@xtra.co.nz
*surrounded by some of the best
trout-fishing rivers in the country*

There are browns up to 4 kg in the confined waters above Long Flat Creek. There are several DoC huts in the upper reaches.

Dingle Burn

The sort of remote mountain stream that draws fly fishers from around the world. They tend to fly in by helicopter but there is also access by boat from Lake Hawea or on the narrow Timaru River road to Dingle Burn Station. There are also several tramping tracks that give access. Permission should be obtained if crossing Dingle Burn or Birchwood Stations. The Dingle holds mainly rainbow up to 2 kg in fast-flowing rocky pools and runs, but its superb mountain location makes it popular with guides and many fish have probably been caught more than once. The most accessible water is in the open tussock flats between Cotters and the Upper Dingle huts.

Timaru River (Creek)

A clear stream that flows into Lake Hawea about 20 km from Hawea township. There is good dry fly and nymph fishing, for both browns and rainbows, about 3 km upstream from the mouth.

Hawea River

The Hawea, which drains Lake Hawea into the Clutha River below Albert Town, holds brown and rainbow trout up to 3.5 kg. Access is reasonable and there is good fishing with dry fly and nymph near the townships of Wanaka and Hawea. It is common to see dry fly hatches and light blue to grey mayflies should always be carried along with some of the beetle imitations for this water. It also fishes well in the evening using caddis.

Clutha River (upper reaches)

The upper Clutha, which drains Lake Wanaka into Lake Dunstan, rarely discolours and drift-dive surveys reveal an exceptionally high trout population, both rainbow and brown. Access is good on both sides of the river, although landowner permission may be needed to get from the highway to some of the best fishing spots. A detailed guide published by the Upper Clutha Angling Club is available at tackle shops in the area. It is not easy to fish during the day when the large trout lie in deep, fast water.

CATCH A MEAL

Skyline Gondola Restaurant
Brecon Street
Queenstown
03 441 0101
www.skyline.co.nz
food with a view

Winnie Bagoes
The Mall
Queenstown
03 442 8635
a Queenstown icon

Fishbone Bar and Grill
7 Beach Street
Queenstown
03 442 6768
seafood in an alpine setting

King George V Coronation Bathhouse Restaurant
Marine Parade
Queenstown
03 442 5625
www.bathhouse.co.nz
stylish use for disused lakefront bathhouse

Relishes Café
99 Ardmore Street
Wanaka
03 443 9018
the locals' favourite

Boardwalk Seafood Restaurant and Bar
Steamer Wharf Village
Queenstown
03 442 5630
boardwalk@xtra.co.nz
succulent seafood on the waterfront

Roaring Megs
57 Shotover Street
03 442 9676
Queenstown
roaringmegs@xtra.co.nz
relaxed dining in an historic setting

Mitchells Tavern
289 South Road
Caversham
Dunedin
03 487 6932
mitchellstavern@xtra.co.nz
close to Carisbrook

Glenfalloch Restaurant
430 Portobello Road
Dunedin
03 476 1006
falloch@xtra.co.nz
set in a 30 acre garden in the Glenfalloch valley

Etrusco at the Savoy
1st Floor, Savoy Building
8A Moray Place
Dunedin
03 477 3737
Italian owned and operated

High Tide Waterfront Restaurant
29 Kitchen Street
Dunedin
03 477 9784
modern food with flair

Bell Pepper Blues
474 Princess Street
Dunedin
03 474 0973
a top chef

But in the evenings when they move into the shallow margins to feed there is excellent wet fly fishing, particularly during the spawning runs.

Lake Dunstan

An artificial lake that holds rainbow and brown trout. Trolling a spinner or smelt fly is the most popular and productive method, although in summer fly fishers can be successful stalking the shoreline.

WAKATIPU DISTRICT

Lake Wakatipu

The South Island's top tourist lake with Queenstown sited midway along it. Wakatipu is large, deep and cold and holds brown and rainbow trout and landlocked quinnat salmon in a sublime mountain setting. Near Queenstown there is good boat fishing using a floating line close to wooded shoes where trout wait for terrestrials falling from the trees. The lake's best-known fishing location is at the head of the lake at Glenorchy where the Rees and Dart Rivers merge into a common delta. In early winter there is good stream-mouth fishing at the Greenstone, Lochy and Von Rivers for trout starting their spawning runs. In summer smelt flies are best at these stream mouths.

Lake Hayes

One of the most photographed lakes in New Zealand, Lakes Hayes, near Queenstown, has good stocks of sizeable brown trout but they are hard to get at because the shorelines are thick with willow trees.

Lakes Kirkpatrick and Moke

Reached from the Glenorchy Road about 7 km from Queenstown, these small lakes in a tussock basin hold brown trout that can be stalked from the shore with a dry fly or damsel nymph.

Diamond Lake

A scenic lake nestled under the eastern flanks of Mount Alfred about 15 km north of Glenorchy. It offers mainly brown trout to shoreline stalking with dry fly or unweighted nymph.

Diamond Creek

Reached by a signposted track soon after crossing the Rees River on the Glenorchy–Paradise Road, this short creek drains the Diamond and Reid Lakes into the Rees River. It is the perfect stream to fish, with clear water and one tussock bank from which fish can be easily spotted. Naturally, it gets heavily fished.

Rees River

Along with the Dart River, the Rees, which drains the Forbes Mountains in Mt Aspiring National Park, is the main water source for Lake Wakatipu. Fishing near the mouth is best late in the season when trout gather for their spawning run.

Route Burn

Another heavily fished stream that flows from the Humboldt Mountains into the Dart River above Glenorchy. Brown and rainbow trout are easily spotted in the clear water but they are also easily spooked.

Greenstone and Caples Rivers

These two popular and heavily fished rivers rise in the Livingstone, Ailsa and Humboldt Mountains before joining to enter the western side of Lake Wakatipu near Elfin Bay. Access is by boat or south from Kinloch on the rough-metalled Greenstone Station Road. The Greenstone–Caples Track – a trek of several days – makes a neat circuit of both rivers which makes it possibly the best wilderness fishing route in the country. The rivers hold browns and rainbows up to 4 kg in clear pools and runs. The best water is the least-fished water – which is that furthest from the road end.

Von River

The Von, which flows into Lake Wakatipu near Mt Nicholas Station, holds rainbow and brown trout. It is best fished early in the season before fish have returned to Lake Wakatipu after spawning. It is reached by boat on the road from Mavora Lakes to Mt Nicholas. The mouth fishes well from April through May.

WHEN THE FISH DON'T BITE

Shotover Jet
PO Box 189
Queenstown
0800 746 868
reservations@shotoverjet.co.nz
www.shotoverjet.com
classic jet-boating thrills

Dart River Safaris
Glenorchy
03 442 9992
info@dartriver.co.nz
www.dartriver.co.nz
jetboat into the heart of the mountains

Dart Stables
Glenorchy
03 442 5688
riding@glenorchy.co.nz
www.glenorchy.co.nz
horse-trekking in paradise

A. J. Hackett Bungy
The Bungy Centre
cnr of Camp and Shotover Streets
Queenstown
03 442 4007
bungyjump@ajhackett.co.nz
www.AJHackett.com
jump with the man who invented bungy

Walter Peak High Country Farm
Fiordland Travel
Queenstown
0800 656 503
www.fiordlandtravel.co.nz
cross Lake Wakatipu in the vintage
steamship, Earnslaw

Gold Trail Tours
22 Kerry Court
Cromwell
03 445 0809
goldtrailtours@xtra.co.nz
in the footsteps of the gold boom

Kingston Flyer
Private Bag
Kingston
Otago
0800 435 937
dgarnett@tranzrail.co.nz
ride a vintage steam train

Taieri Gorge Railway
Railway Station
Anzac Square
Dunedin
03 477 4449
reserve@taieri.co.nz
ride through tunnels and over viaducts on an
historic rail line

Lanarch Castle
Camp Road
Dunedin
03 476 1616
lanarch@lanarchcastle.co.nz
www.lanarchcastle.co.nz
visit New Zealand's only genuine castle

Monarch Wildlife Cruises
cnr Wharf and Fryatt Streets
Dunedin
03 477 4276
monarch@wildlife.co.nz
cruise to Otago Harbour's marine wildlife

Royal Albatross Centre
Taiaroa Head
Otago Peninsula
Dunedin
03 478 0499
reservations@albatrosses.com
www.albatrosses.com
see the world's only mainland albatross
colony

Lochy River

The Lochy reaches Lake Wakatipu at Halfway Bay on the south-western shore and is favoured by Queenstown guides with clients who want a short helicopter ride into a high-country river. Fishers with more dash than cash can get to the mouth by boat or by tramping across mountainous tussock country from the Mt Nicholas Road. Tight restrictions maintain the river's integrity. It is a fly fishing only river, catch-and-release upstream from the Long Burn confluence, and a daily bag of one fish below the Long Burn. There is at least 20 km of fishable water upstream from the mouth best fished by walking and stalking in boots and shorts. Trout are mainly rainbows up to 2.5 kg and will respond to dry fly, nymph and wet fly.

Nevis River

There are few fish in this tributary of the Kawarau River but it has yielded trophy fish to those anglers prepared to put in the time needed walking and stalking. Its headwaters, behind The Remarkables, are reputed to hold brook char.

Southland

There is only one Fish and Game region in New Zealand that before it outlines the fishing attractions in the area asks anglers to leave a fish at the farmhouse occasionally and to put a 'cast' sheep on its feet or notify the farmer concerned. For the enlightenment of those fishers who don't come from Southland, when a pregnant ewe lies down it sometimes is unable to get up again without a bit of help from a shepherd. There is nothing cast about Southland, however. Perhaps slightly eccentric – like the irascible Mayor of Invercargill, Tim Shadbolt – but never prone on the ground.

Southlanders, like their near neighbours the Coasters, are a distinctive, taciturn bunch, and fiercely parochial. You will find them living and working all over New Zealand but their Southland blood runs deep. As is so often the way with émigrés, it is the region of their birth that has shaped them. The rest of the country tends to assume that the bottom end of the South Island is just one step from Antarctica, probably not much warmer and possibly as bleak. In fact, as Shadbolt has been proselytising up and down New Zealand, it is anything but bleak. It is a region that is natural, unspoilt and green. A place without bustle, pollution or high-rise buildings. (A bit like the rest of New Zealand used to be, you might say.)

INFORMATION

Fish and Game New Zealand Southland region
159 North Road
Invercargill
03 215 9117
information@southlandfishgame.co.nz
www.fishandgame.org.nz
Manager: Maurice Rodway
Field Officers: Mark Sutton, Zane Moss, Bill Jarvie (Te Anau) 03 249 8249
Stuart Sutherland (Lumsden) 03 248 7636

Invercargill Visitor Information Centre
Gala Street
Queens Park
03 214 6243
info@southland.org.nz
www.invercargill.org.nz

Toursim Southland
PO Box 903
Invercargill
03 214 9733
tourism@southnet.co.nz

Department of Conservation
State Insurance Building
Don Street
Invercargill
03 214 4589

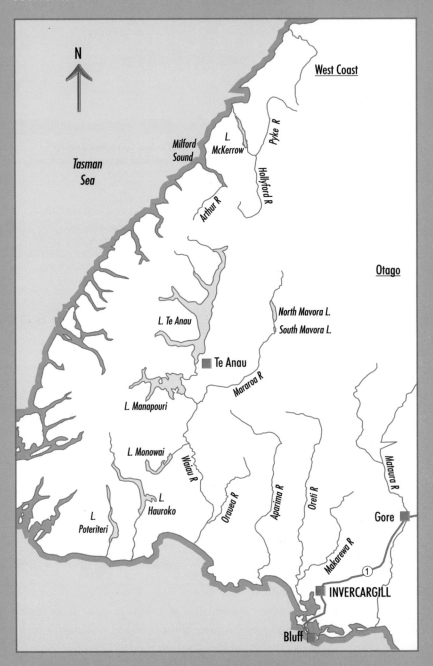

N

West Coast

Tasman
Sea

Milford
Sound

L.
McKerrow

Pyke R

Hollyford R

Arthur R

Otago

L. Te Anau

North Mavora L.

South Mavora L.

Te Anau

Mararoa R

L. Manapouri

L. Monowai

Waiau R

L.
Hauroko

Orauea R

Aparima R

Oreti R

Mataura R

L.
Poteriteri

Gore

Makarewa R

1

INVERCARGILL

Bluff

FAMOUS FOR

- Mayor Tim Shadbolt
- Aluminium smelter
- The Catlins
- Lake Manapouri
- Bluff oysters

- Stewart Island/Rakiura
- Fiordland
- Kepler Track
- Hokonui Moonshine whiskey
- Percy Burn wooden viaduct

It is also the sort of place where farmers don't mind anglers crossing their land to get to top fishing waters – and anglers are equally happy to repay the hospitality with a fish and to help a cast sheep back on its feet.

Trout fishing in Southland is as fresh and untouched as the region. The Mataura River is an internationally renowned fishery that attracts anglers from around the world to cast a fly at its brown trout. The insect hatch on the Mataura's evening rise sends trout into a feeding frenzy – and fly fishers into a frenzy too, trying to match the hatch with the right artificial to tempt the trout. But it's not easy because during its evening hatch the mayfly goes through three phases – the hatching nymph, the moult case from the immature insect, and the adult female that, having laid its eggs, falls to the surface and is soon to die. It is a brown trout banquet, and one that the purist trout fishermen of Southland and their visitors from overseas talk about in hushed tones.

Besides the Mataura, which has about 150 km of fishable water, there are more than 27 quality fishing rivers and streams. The Southland freshwater fishing region also includes Fiordland, which not only contains some challenging fishing waters but is unrivalled for its scenic magic. On the opposite coast is the Catlins region where seals, penguins and sea lions play on the bush-fringed coastline. Bluff, with its famous oysters, is supposed to be as far south as you can go in New Zealand but, of course, it's not. Just across Foveaux Strait is Stewart Island/Rakiura and the country's newest national park – Rakiura National Park.

WHERE AND WHAT

Fish and Game New Zealand's Southland region covers the bottom of the South Island with its western district encompassing all of Fiordland as far north as the Cascade River.

There are four major river systems in the region. The Mataura and Oreti Rivers have their headwaters in the high country south of Lake Wakatipu. The Waiau River drains Lakes Te Anau and Manapouri, and the Aparimu River begins in the Takitimu Mountains. The four rivers flow south across the Southland plains into Foveaux Strait.

Brown trout, introduced in 1870, predominate to the extent that Gore can safely call itself the trout-fishing capital of New Zealand without being too much at odds with the rival claim of Turangi, in the North Island, where rainbow trout rule. There is a variety of fishing waters in Fiordland, a World Heritage area, although the fishing is mostly wilderness fishing in remote areas. Rarely visited headwater streams will likely hold trophy-size fish.

The Southland region's regulations follow the general South Island regulations, although waters in the region are mostly subject to quite detailed seasonal restrictions on legal fishing methods. The fishing season is linked to the method of fishing and the conditions on a Southland licence need to be carefully studied.

Lakes open all year to artificial flies and lures are Lakes Ada, Alabaster, Hauroko, Manapouri, McKerrow, Monowai, North Mavora, Poteriteri, South Mavora, and Te Anau. The lower sections of some rivers are open all year. These are the Mataura, between the mouth and the Gorge Road bridge; the Oreti River from the mouth to the Riverton–Invercargill highway; the

Titiroa River downstream of the Locks; the Waiau River from the mouth to the Tuatapere Bridge; the Waihopai River downstream of Queens Drive; the Waikawa from the mouth to Niagara Bridge; the Makarewa downstream from the Riverton–Invercargill highway; the Aparima from the mouth to the Thornbury Bridge; the Waimatuku Stream downstream of Rance Road; and the Waikiwi Stream downstream of North Road bridge. All rivers and streams flowing into the Tasman Sea are also open all year round.

There is a closed season from 30 April to 1 October on the Aparima, Mararoa, Mataura (upper), Mokoreta (Wyndham), Monowai, Orauea, Oreti, Pourakino, Titiroa (upstream of the Locks), Waiau (upper), Makarewa (upper), Waihopai (upper), Waikaia, Waikawa, Wairaki and Whitestone Rivers; Acton, Mimihau, Irthing, Otamita, Otautau, Waikiwi (upper), Waimatuku (upper), Waimea, Morley and Waikaka Streams; Borland, Lill and Hamilton Burns; and Lakes Thomas and Waituna.

The closed season is 31 May to 1 November on all tributaries of Lakes Te Anau, Manapouri, Monowai, Hauroko and Hankinson; the Eglinton and Upukerora Rivers; Lakes Fergus, Gunn, and Hankinson. The Eglinton River is restricted to fly fishing only.

The region has a catch-and-release zone on the Oreti River and tributaries from the headwaters to the downstream limit of the 'walk only zone'; and the Mataura River and tributaries upstream of the road bridge at Garston.

The daily limit elsewhere in the region is four trout. There is no restriction on fish length.

Casting 🐟 around

ORETI RIVER

This major Southland river has varied access on both banks for its entire
length. A series of side roads lead to the river and there are many marked
anglers' access tracks. Where permission is required to cross farmland it is
usually readily given.

In its upper reaches the Oreti, which rises in the Thomson Mountains,
holds some large fish that are a challenge for the fly fisher prepared to walk
and stalk the shingle beds. The fish are shy and the river is exposed to
prevailing winds, making fishing difficult. Further downstream, between
Mossburn and Centre Bush, the river becomes slightly braided and fish are
difficult to see. There are good fish stocks but the glides and riffles mostly
have to be fished blind. Below Winton, spin fishing is more effective than fly
fishing. The tidal section is heavily fished, mostly from boats. Some huge
sea-run browns have been caught here.

MARAROA RIVER

The Mararoa has its headwaters between the Thomson and Livingstone
Mountains and flows into and out of the Mavora Lakes before joining the
Whitestone River and thence into Lake Manapouri via the Waiau River.
Above Mavora Lakes the river holds both brown and rainbow trout. This is
wilderness fishing to sighted fish. Below Mavora Lakes there is excellent
fishing, again both brown and rainbow, with surveys revealing good
numbers of fish.

The lower section of the river is reached at the Mararoa bridge and also
from the road to Manapouri that turns off the Te Anau highway. Three km
along this road is the Whitestone River bridge. Access is available here to the
Whitestone/Mararoa/Flaxy Creek junction which is about 800 m
downstream from the bridge. Continue west for 8.5 km past the Whitestone
River bridge to where there is a left turn onto Manapouri–Redcliff Road,
which leads to a bridge over the lower Mararoa River and gives access to its

junction with the Waiau River and the Mararoa Weir. There is reasonable fishing in these waters for boots-and-shorts anglers.

MATAURA RIVER

There is good access from both banks of the Mataura for much of its length although in places landowner permission is required. The east bank is easily reached near Wyndham and between Mataura and Gore. The next bridge access upstream is near Riversdale on the Riversdale–Waikaia Road and good fishing can be had in this area. Detailed access information for the Mataura is given in a free Fish and Game guide available from tackle shops and information centres in Southland.

The upper section of the Mataura holds reasonable numbers of moderate-sized browns. In the summer when it is daylight in Southland until about 10 pm, mayflies hatch during the warm evenings and trout will rise vigorously to feed on them. The middle reaches, between Gore and Cattle Flat, is the most popular section of the river. It is slow and meandering across farmland, and while trout can be hard to spot unless rising, the numbers are high. This is the main area fished during the mad Mataura rise. Below Gore the Mataura is larger and deeper and fish can be difficult to see as the water begins to lose its clarity.

TACKLE BOX

Bert Walker SportsWorld
147 Dee Street
Invercargill
03 218 9025

Sportsexpress
65 Main Street
Gore
03 208 0801

Stirling Sports
28 Esk Street
Invercargill
03 214 9235

Te Anau Sportsworld
38–40 Town Centre
Te Anau
03 249 8195

WAIKAIA RIVER

The Waikaia, a major tributary of the Mataura, has its origins in Central Otago, flowing south for more than 50 km before joining the Mataura near Riversdale. There is access to both banks from the Freshford Bridge a few kilometres from Riversdale. Between this bridge and Waikaia township the road runs beside the river and there are a number of signposted access points. Above Piano Flat there is limited access from Whitecombe Road which is a dry weather only road.

The Waikaia has an excellent reputation as a brown trout fishery, particularly in the middle and lower reaches where the pools and runs are long and access is good. The banks are often willow-lined, and a willow grub imitation can at times be lethal.

APARIMA RIVER

A medium-sized river that begins in the Takitimu Mountains and reaches the sea near Riverton. It has a good brown trout population and is a pleasant river to fish. The middle and upper reaches provide good fly fishing. Spin fishing is usually preferable as the river nears the sea. There is good water at Hazlett's Crossing which is reached by travelling along the Thornbury–Isla Bank road for 4 km, and down Hazlett Road. Further north along Hazlett's at the Fairfax Bridge there is a popular fishing, swimming and picnic spot. Upstream from Otautau, Munro Road leads to a gravel track that accesses

GUIDES AND CHARTERS

Alan Wilson
411 Herbert Street
Invercargill
03 217 3687
dryfly@southnet.co.nz
www.fishnz.net.nz

Dennis Collins
9 Baird Street
Invercargill
03 2172890

Michael Bednar
40 Cathedral Drive
Manapouri
03 249 6996
bednar@es.co.nz
www.flyfishnz.com

Murray Knowles
PO Box 84
Te Anau
03 249 7565
sthguide@southnet.co.nz

Dean Bell
PO Box 198
Te Anau
03 249 7847
deanbell@xtra.co.nz

Daniel Agar
PO Box 47
Mataura
03 442 4373
daniel@mataura-flyfishing.com
www.mataura-flyfishing.com

John Hannabus
23 Milton Street
Gore
03 208 4922
fishing@esi.co.nz
www.browntrout.co.nz

Bryan Burgess
6 Mitre Street
Gore
03 208 0801
bunny.helen@burges.co.nz
www.bbsports.co.nz

David Murray-Orr
PO Box 111
Gore
southlandflies@hotmail.com
www.mataura.co.nz

some excellent water. There is also good fishing near Otautau from the west bank. Because it is fed from a small catchment the Aparima often remains fishable when others have become flooded.

WAIAU RIVER

The Manapouri power scheme changed the flow of the Waiau but it still fishes reasonably well. Both banks can be reached from a number of places. Some particularly beautiful water is easily accessed near Monowai. On the west bank there are several access points to good water near Dean Forest. On the upper Waiau there is some excellent fishing near Manapouri.

CATCH A MEAL

The Cabbage Tree
379 Dunns Road
Otatara
Invercargill
03 213 1443
cabbage.tree@xtra.co.nz
www.thecabbagetree.com
fine food and wine

Waxy O'Sheas Irish Pub
Dee Street
Invercargill
03 214 0313
Irish pub dining

Thai Dee
9 Dee Street
Invercargill
03 214 5112
authentic Thai food

Birchwoods Restaurant
cnr Racecourse Road and Tay Street
Invercargill
03 217 6195
ascot@ilt.co.nz
à la carte dining

Lone Star Café and Bar
cnr Leet and Dee Streets
Invercargill
03 214 6225
lonestar@southnet.co.nz
an atmosphere you can taste

Molly O'Grady's
cnr Kelvin and Esk Streets
Invercargill
03 218 2829
kelvin@ilt.co.nz
Irish theme restaurant and bar

Big Willy's 'Cook Your Own'
Newfield Tavern
Centre Street
Invercargill
03 216 7313
newfield@southnet.co.nz
you choose, you cook

Bracken Hall
33 Devon Street
Mossburn
03 248 6033
gateway to Fiordland

HANG YOUR HOOK

Kowhai Lodge
5664 Highway 94
c/o Post Office
Mossburn–Te Anau Highway
03 248 6137
top fishing on the Oreti River which forms one boundary of the property

Gore Stream Cottage
2057 Tahakopa Valley Road
RD2 Owaka
Tahakopa
Catlins Region
03 415 894
hosts@gorgestream.co.nz
www.gorgestream.co.nz
nestled in the heart of the Catlins beside its own stream

Murrell's Grand View House
7 Murrell Avenue
Manapouri
03 249 6642
murrell@xtra.co.nz
colonial guesthouse restored to its former ambience

Castlerock Cookhouse
Castlerock Road
RD2 Lumsden
Southland
03 248 7435
cookhse@xtra.co.nz
self-contained accommodation in restored 1870s station concrete cookhouse

Smith's Farmstay
365 Wyndham–Mokoreta Road
Wyndham
Southland
03 206 4840
beverly@smithsfarmstay.co.nz
a fisherman's retreat where the host will share his knowledge of local rivers

Argyll Farmstay
Rapid No 246
Clutha River Road
Balclutha
03 415 9269
argyllfm@ihug.co.nz
sited on the banks of the Clutha River where the farm's own jet-boat will take you fishing

Mount Prospect Station
Kakapo Road
Te Anau
03 249 7082
on-site trout fishing in the Whitestone River

Mainholm Lodge
Pomaka Road
Tapanui
03 204 8024
mainholm@xtra.co.nz
in the heart of brown trout country

Blackhills Farmstay
197 Roberston Road
North Chatton
RD3 Gore
03 207 2865
six fishing rivers within 30 minutes of this 360 ha sheep farm

Alstead Farmstay
173 Neill Road
Tokanui
03 246 8804
fish the Mataura and Waikawa Rivers from this hospitable homestay

McRae Homestay
143A Broughton Street
Gore
03 208 0662
the rivers close by are world-renowned for trout fishing

FIORDLAND RIVERS AND LAKES

Hollyford River

Wild and scenic with browns up to 4.5 kg, the Hollyford must rate as one of the most spectacular wilderness rivers in New Zealand. Adventurous anglers who fish the Hollyford can use a number of DoC huts.

Lake McKerrow

The lake fills a drowned glacial valley, with bush running down to the shoreline. It is best fished using spinning gear.

Pyke River

The Pyke, which joins the Hollyford about 6 km from Lake McKerrow, is a good river for wild brown trout – but you have to tramp to get there.

Arthur River

The famed Milford Track follows the Arthur soon after it tumbles over the Sutherland Falls. It holds good-sized browns but its fish get a lot of inquisitive attention from trekkers. It is likely easier to fish Lake Ada, which the Arthur flows into and out of, from a boat – an option that a guiding company makes available to track walkers.

Clinton River

The Milford Track follows the Clinton to its headwaters at McKinnon Pass. It is unbelievably clear and its pools hold easily seen fish of trophy size. Catching them is quite another thing. It is likely that Clinton trout spend as much time looking at Milford Track walkers as the

HANG YOUR HOOK

Southern Home Hospitality
Rimu Rural No. 375
RD1 Invercargill
Southland
03 230 4798
home-hosp@hotmail.com
home baking and famous trout rivers within easy reach

Lands End NZ
Stirling Pt
State Highway 1
Bluff
03 212 7575
landsend@southnet.co.nz
bed and breakfast furthest south

Tudor Park Farmstay
21 Lawrence Road
Royal Bush
RD6 Invercargill
03 221 7150
janemckay@xtra.co.nz
tranquil setting close to Invercargill

WHEN THE FISH DON'T BITE

Doubtful Sound tour
Fiordland Travel
0800 656 502
manapouri1@fiordlandtravel.co.nz

Catlins Coastal Heritage Trail
Trail brochures available from information
centres
half-day walk past sea-lions and penguins to
the South Island's most southern point

Nugget Point EcoTours
Nugget View Motel
Kaka Pt
South Otago
03 412 8602
nugview@catlins.co.nz
www.catlins.co.nz
cruise past teeming birdlife and marine
mammals

Catlins Wildlife Trackers
RD2 Papatowai
Owaka
South Otago
03 415 8613
catlinw@es.co.nz
wildlife walks

Tiwai Pt Aluminium Smelter
Tiwai Pt
Invercargill
03 218 5999
www.comalco.com.au
guided tours of the country's biggest
electricity user

Fiordland Wilderness Experiences
66 Quintin Drive
Te Anau
03 249 7768
fiordland.sea.kayak@clear.net.nz
www.fiordlandseakayak.co.nz
guided sea-kayaking in the sounds and lakes
of Fiordland

Fiordland Helicopters
Te Anau Airport
Te Anau
03 249 7575
information@fiordlandhelicopters.co.nz
drop in to a rugged, untamed wilderness

Milford Sound Sea Kayaks
Paddle on Inn
Deepwater Basin
Milford Sound
0800 476 726
rosco@kayakmilford.co.nz
www.kayakmilford.co.nz
see Milford Sound's wildlife at water level

Submarine Adventures
Town Centre
Milford Sound
03 474 1783
info@submarines.co.na
www.submarines.co.nz
Milford Sound from 250 m down

Adventure Charters
33 Waiau Street
Manapouri
03 249 6626
information@fiordlandadventure.co.nz
www.fiordlandadventure.co.nz
Doubtful Sound by guided sea kayak

Sinbad Cruises
15 Fergus Square
Te Anau
03 249 7106
sinbad@teanau.co.nz
cruise Lake Te Anau on a gaff-rigged
wooden ketch

Waterwings Airways Te Anau
Lakefront Drive
Te Anau
03 249 7405
waterwings@teanau.co.nz
travel by floatplane in to remote reaches

trekkers do ogling giant trout. Most walkers who carry a fly rod for a flick along the way, leave the Clinton Valley empty-handed.

Worsley Stream

A remote stream in rugged bush country holding large rainbow trout. It is best suited to those who like to combine tramping with angling.

Eglinton River

The Eglinton, which flows down the Eglinton Valley into Lake Te Anau, is restricted to fly fishing only. It holds mainly rainbow trout that are easily spotted in pools and runs. Good fishing water is easy for anglers to reach.

Lake Te Anau

Te Anau is the largest lake in the South Island. It is best fished trolling from a boat. A detailed access guide to these waters is available from Fish and Game Southland region.

Upper Waiau River

This section of the Waiau, between Lake Te Anau and Lake Manapouri, has a good stock of rainbow trout and is easy to fish using spin fishing gear.

Lake Monowai

Trolling is really the only option for this lake, which has been affected by the Manapouri power scheme and is surrounded by dense bush.

Lake Hauroko

An exposed lake to the south of Monowai that is best suited to trolling, although there are some shallow bays where cruising brown trout can be stalked.

The Sports Fishing Regulations

These regulations are set to ensure that the fisheries are protected for future generations. At the same time they aim to maintain the quality of the fishing experience. The main rules are shown here but there are other rules in the Conservation Act, Freshwater Fisheries regulations and others which also affect sports fishing. If you are in any doubt about sports fishing regulations please contact your local Fish and Game Office.

Fresh water anglers enjoy a special privilege because they have the responsibility to manage and protect New Zealand's sports fishery. Every three years whole season adult licence holders elect the 144 councillors on the 12 regional fish and game councils to manage sports fish and game on their behalf. These regulations are not set by a faceless bureaucracy – but by elected anglers. They review the results of the monitoring of fish stocks and harvest rates, consult with clubs and interested anglers and then recommend to the Minister of Conservation regulations they believe best protect, and make more enjoyable, the fishing in their region.

The licence fee is not related to the cost of managing a particular area. Rather it is each angler's part contribution towards the total cost of managing fish and game and promoting the interests of anglers and hunters nationally.

NATIONAL REGULATIONS (FIRST SCHEDULE) – apply to all regions.

1. Interpretation

Words and expressions in this notice which are defined in the Conservation Act 1987 or the Freshwater Fisheries Regulations 1983, shall be so defined.

'All year' means a 12 month period commencing on 1 October and concluding on 30 September of the following year, both days inclusive.

'Artificial fly' means any lure of feather, fur, wool or other material of any kind customarily used in the making of artificial flies; but shall not include any lure in the tying of which lead or other weight has been incorporated unless the hook incorporated in that lure does not exceed 14 mm in length (exclusive of the eye) and the gape of the hook does not exceed 6 mm.

'Bait' means:
Natural fly
Natural insect
Natural spider
Natural worm or worms
Natural crustacea
Natural fish (excluding fish ova, or any portion of a fish, or shellfish [mollusca])
Uncoloured bread dough.

'Bait Assembly' means either a hook rigged with a number of baits, or a single bait rigged with a number of hooks.

'Bait Fishing' means to fish for sports fish with bait.

'Boat' means any manned flotation device.

'Fishing' and 'fish' in this Notice means:
(a) The catching, taking, or harvesting of sports fish; and
(b) Includes
    (i) Any other activity that may reasonably be expected to result in the catching, taking, or harvesting of sports fish;
    (ii) Any attempt to catch, take or harvest sports fish;
    (iii) Any operation in support of, or in preparation for, any activity described in this definition.

'Foulhook' means to hook a sports fish otherwise than from within the mouth.

'Length' is the measurement from the tip of the snout to the fork of the tail.

'Lure' means any authorised artificial fly, or spinner, or bait.

'Spinner' means any artificial lure other than an artificial fly.

'Spin Fishing' means to fish for sports fish with a spinner.

'Sports fish' means those freshwater fish described in the First Schedule of the Freshwater Fisheries Regulations 1983, namely:

Brown Trout

Rainbow trout

American brook trout or char

Lake trout or char

Atlantic salmon

Quinnat or chinook salmon

Sockeye salmon

Perch

Tench

Rudd (Auckland/Waikato region only).

2. Authorised tackle

2.1 No licence holder shall fish for sports fish except by using a rod and running line and authorised lure.

2.2 Nets:

2.2.1 When playing a sports fish a landing net may be used to secure or land that fish.

2.2.2 For keeping non-salmonid sports fish alive, a keep net may be used in the water from which the fish was caught.

2.3 No licence holder shall use more than one assembled rod and running line.

2.4 No licence holder shall fish for sports fish unless within 15 m of the rod being used.

2.5 No licence holder when fishing for sports fish shall use more than one bait assembly.

3. Foul hooking of fish

3.1 No licence holder shall attempt to foul hook any sports fish.

3.2 Any licence holder who foul hooks a sports fish shall return it immediately to the water with as little injury as possible.

4. Minimum and maximum length

Every licence holder who catches a sports fish which does not exceed the specified minimum length, or does exceed the specified maximum length, shall immediately return it with as little injury as possible into the water from which it was taken.

5. Open season

No licence holder shall fish for any sports fish except during an open season.

6. Daily limit bags

6.1 No licence holder shall continue to fish for a particular species of sports fish on any day in which he or she has already killed the limit bag for that species except in Otago (see Second Schedule).

6.2 It shall be permissible to make up the difference between a lesser limit bag prescribed in one place and a higher limit bag prescribed in another.

7. Authorised lures and baits

Authorised lures and baits (subject to any regional restrictions specified in the Second Schedule) are:

Artificial fly
Spinner
Bait.

catch your trout
and eat it, too

Incredible as it may seem, there are serious anglers who never eat the trout they catch. Just why anyone would kill such a fine creature if they don't intend to put it to a worthy use seems a tragic waste.

Trout has a subtle flavour and deserves to be prepared for a meal with the same care and attention that is devoted to catching it. The flavour is easily ruined if the trout is not gutted fairly quickly with the blood cavity along the backbone cleaned out, gills removed, and all trace of scales and slime scraped off the skin.

Simplicity is often best. One of my most memorable trout fishing experiences goes back some years ago when I was part of a display of corporate extravagance that involved flying a group of us – including a London business-man – from Auckland to Taupo where we were collected by fishing guide and charter operator Simon Dickie and taken to the Taupo lake front. From there a float plane flew us to the southern end of the lake where Dickie's partner was waiting with a launch.

By 8.10 am the first trout was on board. At 1 pm the float plane returned for us and I was back in my Auckland office by 3 pm – with two nice rainbow trout in the boot of the car.

But the highlight of this perfect day was, without doubt, our lunch. While we fished the skipper took one of the morning's catch and filleted, skinned and boned it. The fillets were then lightly pan-fried in butter, along with a little lemon, and served with a simple salad and chilled white wine. Superb.

There are as many ways to serve trout as there are any fish. Some people even preserve their catch by bottling it at high temperatures. After a few months it looks – and tastes – like salmon. Frankly, I don't think it worth the effort – or worthy of the trout. Better to buy a can of Canadian salmon and save bottling for the day you catch a boat load of kahawai – sea trout – which will also look and taste like salmon after a few months.

On occasions when we do have trout that we want to keep for future consumption, I prepare the fish for quick smoking by removing the head, stomach lining and bones but keeping the two fillets joined by the skin at the backbone as this will enhance eventual presentation.

Then I place a piece of cling film between the two sides of the fish before folding them back together and freezing it. Our trout is then ready to become a dinner party entrée at fairly quick notice using my wife's 'quick smoke' recipe.

Fran's Hot Smoked Trout

Take one trout boned out, rub in salt, pepper, brown sugar and dark rum (or sherry or whisky). Smoke lightly in a portable smoker according to the manufacturer's instructions and serve whole with French bread or crackers.

On the Riverbank

Anglers fishing the wilderness can augment their rations with trout cooked according to several streamside recipes. The first essential is a good bed of hot coals produced from a fire made from an aromatic wood such as manuka. Then use the traditional Boy Scout technique of steam-baking your gutted and cleaned fish by wrapping it in copious pages of sopping wet newspaper (or clay) and burying it in the embers. You can choose to include some herbs of your choice before wrapping it up, if you like. By the time the outer layers of newspaper have burned away your trout will be well cooked in its own juices and ready to eat – preferably with lashings of black pepper, salt and fresh bread.

By using a wire grill, you can also cook a trout on an open fire. Prepare the fish by rubbing lots of butter and pepper into the flesh before placing it in the grill. Serve with a green salad, some fresh bread and chilled beer. Delicious!